OUTDOOR EDUCATION AT SCHOOL

OUTDOOR EDUCATION AT SCHOOL

PRACTICAL ACTIVITIES AND PROBLEM-SOLVING LESSONS

SECOND EDITION

GARRY POWELL

amba press

Copyright © Garry Powell 2023

All rights reserved. No part of this book may be reproduced or transmitted in any form or by any means, electronic or mechanical, including photocopying, recording or by any information storage and retrieval system, without prior permission in writing from the publisher.

First published in 1987
This second edition is published in 2023

Published by Amba Press
Melbourne, Australia
www.ambapress.com.au

Cover designer – Tess McCabe
Illustrator – Cathy Larsen

We thank Cathy Larsen for the permission to reuse her beautiful original illustrations.

ISBN: 9781922607423 (pbk)
ISBN: 9781922607430 (ebk)

A catalogue record for this book is available from the National Library of Australia.

CONTENTS

Introduction	1
Levels 1 and 2: Fifteen Lessons	**3**
Environmental Awareness	4
Trailing	8
Mapping	10
Safety	13
Problem-solving	14
Levels 3 and 4: Twenty-four Lessons	**19**
Environmental Studies	20
Trailing	24
Safety	29
Mapping	30
Ropes	39
Problem-solving	42
Level 5: Twenty-five Lessons	**47**
Environmental Studies	48
Mapping	54
Navigation	62
Ropes	68
Bushcraft	70
Level 6: Thirty Lessons	**73**
Environmental Studies	74
Mapping	79
Navigation	88

Level 7: Thirty-five Lessons	**97**
Navigation	99
Initiative Activities	111
Signalling	114
Bushcraft	120
Ropes	124
Appendix – Knots	137
Appendix – Compass Games	141
Subject Index	151

INTRODUCTION

Time spent in an outdoor environment whether it be a backyard, school ground, local park or natural forest; has been proved to ease stress, improve sensory awareness and give a feeling of freedom.

Outdoor education is the activities and learning done to prepare the student **for** the outdoors. It is done by creating an interest **in** and developing a body of knowledge **about** the outdoors. It teaches skills that promote safety in and a positive appreciation of the outdoor environment.

It should take place as an integral part of the general school program rather than a specific area of study. Each curriculum area can have an outdoor education component.

A comprehensive outdoor education program can be conducted entirely **at school**, using the classroom, a clear indoor area (such as a gymnasium) and the school ground.

Follow up activities done on excursion at a nearby park or on a base camp are regarded as part of an **extension** program.

Outdoor education can develop:
- Skills and knowledge that lead to a lifelong involvement in worthwhile leisure pursuits.
- Promote aspects of personal development, self-esteem, resourcefulness, independence, leadership, cooperation, judgement and tolerance.
- Responsible attitudes towards personal and group safety in an outdoor environment.
- Appreciation of the impact of human behaviour on the overall environment.

The lessons in this book contain activities from all areas of the primary school curriculum.

They include: sensory skills, observation, problem solving, awareness of nature, safety, maps, rope activities, navigation, trailing, bushcraft, environmental studies, initiative activities, signalling.

The lessons are not organised in grade levels but in developmental progression from simple and introductory to complex.

Examples:
- Level 1 and 2 mapping should be done before Levels 3, 4, 5, 6 mapping and so on.
- Lessons for Foundation and Grade 1 classes taking outdoor education for the first time could perhaps be restricted to Level 1 and 2 – Lessons 1, 2, 3, 4, 7, 13 and 14.
- Whereas a Grade 1 having completed these lessons in their Foundation year might revise those done in Foundation and then do Level 1 and 2 – Lessons 5, 6, 8, 9, 10, 11, 12 and 15.
- A Grade 6 doing outdoor education for the first time might take mostly lessons from Levels 1 and 2, a few from Levels 3 and 4 and a couple more from Levels 5, 6 and 7.
- Likewise, students from Years 7, 8 and 9 doing outdoor education for the first time might take lessons from all levels.
- When students have followed this outdoor education program for their six previous years, it's then that they will be able to complete and enjoy the tasks set in Level 7.

LEVELS 1 AND 2

No.	Legend	Theme	Subject
1.	♣	Environmental Awareness	Sensory
2.	♣	Environmental Awareness	Sensory
3.	♣	Environmental Awareness	Rules When Walking
4.	♣	Environmental Awareness	Observation
5.		Trailing	Techniques
6.		Trailing	Set Trail in Pairs
7.		Mapping	Home
8.		Mapping	School
9.		Mapping	Observation Walk
10.		Safety	Rules in the Bush
11.	💡	Problem-solving	Develop Thinking
12.	💡	Problem-solving	All Aboard
13.	💡	Problem-solving	Poisonous Jelly
14.	💡	Problem-solving	Auditory Direction
15.	💡	Problem-solving	Unnatural

LEVELS 1 AND 2 **LESSON 1**

ENVIRONMENTAL AWARENESS: SENSORY

Aim
To develop sensory awareness – the sense of touch.

Equipment
- 6 blindfolds
- Adventure playground

Warm Up
Here, There, Where
Three stations called Here, There and Where are selected. On the call 'Here', 'There' or 'Where', the group runs quickly to the respective station.

Introduction
Discuss the use of sight in the bush environment. Consider other senses that may be valuable in the bush:
- Touch
- Smell
- Hearing
- Taste.

Activity
In the classroom, have the students identify objects while blindfolded.

In pairs in the playground have students use other senses to identify things while blindfolded. For example:
- Touch – grass, stones, concrete, wood, metal
- Hear – birds, cards, people walking
- Smell – grass, flowers, smoke, fumes.

LEVELS 1 AND 2   LESSON 2

ENVIRONMENTAL AWARENESS: SENSORY

Aim
To develop sensory awareness – the senses of touch and hearing.

Equipment
- 6 blindfolds
- Adventure playground

Warm Up
Bombers and Fighters
'Bombers' are formed by two players joining hands and moving freely within a confined area. Three or four players become 'fighters' and attempt to shoot down the 'bombers' by tagging them. Once a 'bomber' is tagged it must stand still and make an archway by holding hands above their heads. It can be freed to re-join the game by another 'bomber' flying through the archway.

Introduction
Revise the use of senses and their application in a bush environment:
- Touch
- Smell
- Hearing
- Taste
- Sight.

Activity
In pairs – the visual partner leads the blindfolded around a designated part of the playground.

Remove blindfolds and have the students indicate the route which was taken.

LEVELS 1 AND 2   *LESSON 3*

ENVIRONMENTAL AWARENESS: RULES WHEN WALKING

Aim

To develop a knowledge of rules when walking.

Warm Up

Circle Tag

Two circles of four students join hands. Keeping hands joined each circle chases the remainder of the group. Any player touched by the arms or shoulders of anyone from the chasing circle joins the circle. The idea is to form a circle of seven students.

Introduction

Discuss the importance of walking as a part of physical fitness and as a recreational pastime.

Rules For Walking

1. Never walk alone.
2. Always tell parents or someone in authority where you are going and your expected time of arrival.
3. Use a 'leader' and a 'whip'.
4. Keep together.

Activity

Appoint a leader and a whip and walk around the schoolgrounds. Observe points of environmental interest while walking. Ensure that the four rules of walking are obeyed.

LEVELS 1 AND 2 — LESSON 4

ENVIRONMENTAL AWARENESS: OBSERVATION

Aim
To promote an awareness of the environment.

Equipment
- Coloured bibs or braids

Warm Up
Catch Your Partner's Tail
Each student chases their partner and tries to catch the tucked in, coloured bib or braid. Change partners and repeat.

Introduction
Discuss the need for an awareness of the environment. Walk around the school block. Distinguish between seeing and observing.

Activity
Stop and observe trees, grasses, shadows, insects, birds, power-poles etc.

Discuss and classify according to type, size, formation, construction.

LEVELS 1 AND 2 **LESSON 5**

TRAILING: TECHNIQUES

Aim
To develop track/trail techniques.

Equipment
- A trail which has been marked out by chalk or tape around part of the schoolground.
- Other equipment to be collected on the walk, e.g., stones, sticks, etc.

Warm Up
Jump the Moving Snake
Partner A wiggles a rope like a snake on the ground. Partner B jumps the snake so as not to be bitten.

Introduction
Discuss the basic types of trails:
- Visual – follow arrows made with chalk, tape, sticks, stones, etc.
- Written – clues written and placed at successive stops/sites.

Activities
Walk around the schoolground following a pre-marked trail.

TIED GRASS.   TWIG ARROW.   GROUP OF STONES.

LEVELS 1 AND 2   LESSON 6

TRAILING:
SET TRAIL IN PAIRS

Aim
To develop the ability to set a suitable trail for others to follow.

Equipment
- Chalk for trail

Warm Up
Leap Frog Run
Partner A stands in a bent position low enough for Partner B to leap frog over. B runs behind A, leap frogs over.

Introduction
Revise methods of laying trail. Discuss unsatisfactory trail blazing methods (scratching in the ground, chalk on trees, charcoal messages). Set the situation 'Lost in the Bush'. Revise rules for walking.

Activity
One pair sets a trail for another pair. This involves marking the ground with their sign (e.g. a bird footprint) so that the other pair can follow the trail. Between the start and finish of the trail there should be a set number (e.g. three) of stations (controls). Each station is marked by a control which is both numbered and coded. The number ensures that the 'seekers' follow the trail in order, whereas the code, when recorded enables the 'setters' to check that the 'seekers' have completed the course.

LEVELS I AND 2 **LESSON 7**

MAPPING: HOME

Aim

To be able to draw the plan of your home.

Equipment

- Room with tables and chairs
- Paper
- Coloured pencils

Warm Up

Chase Your Number

Four teams are needed. Each team is arranged along the side of a square. Each member is given a number and when this number is called that student chases their counterpart from the other team, in an anticlockwise direction, around the square. Call new numbers frequently to ensure that everyone has lots of activity.

Introduction

Explain the concept of a 'plan', drawing one on cardboard or whiteboard.

Activity

Students draw the rooms of their house one at a time, adding on each new room when directed. Count the number of rooms. Colour-code the different rooms, e.g. bedrooms – red; kitchen – green; bathroom – blue.

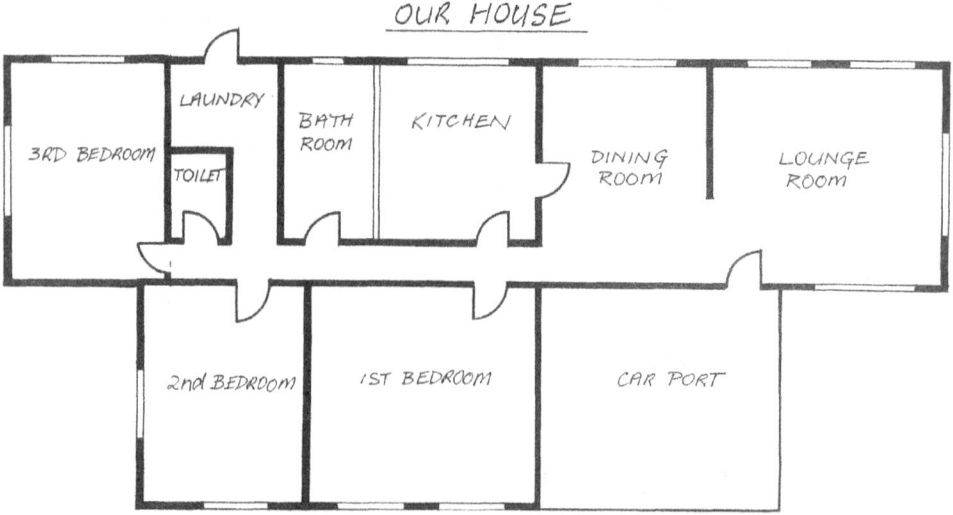

LEVELS 1 AND 2
LESSON 8

MAPPING: SCHOOL

Aim
To be able to read a map.

Equipment
- Stencilled or duplicated map of an environmental walk, e.g. streets surrounding the school.

Warm Up
Change Bases
Around a circle of about six metres in diameter, mark about six evenly spaced bases. A player stands at each of the six bases and a player, who is 'it', stands at the centre of the circle. When the supervisor calls out 'change' the players around the circle must change bases and 'it' tries to capture one. A foot resting on a base determines capture.

Introduction
Distribute copies of the map to the students and discuss the directions and the various 'stations' along the walk.

Activity
Colour the map showing the route of the walk, picking out the 'stations' in contrasting colour. Collect the maps for the next session.

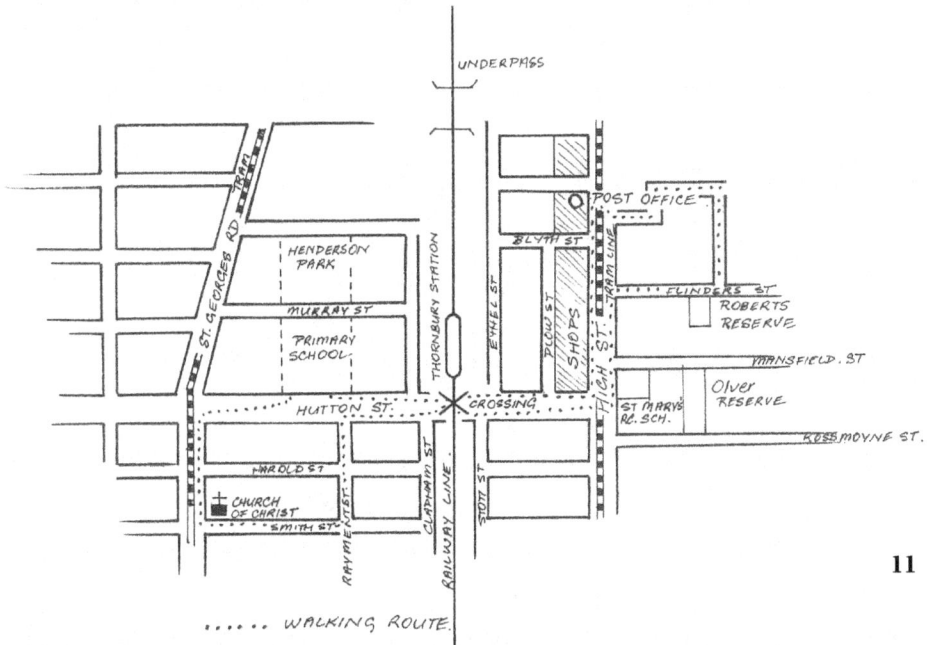

LEVELS 1 AND 2   LESSON 9

MAPPING:
OBSERVATION WALK OF SCHOOLGROUND

Aim

To develop an awareness of what is involved in the environment of the school: ground surfaces, play equipment, plants, vistas.

Equipment
- Maps
- Papers (worksheets)
- Pencils

Introduction

Distribute the maps to the students and revise the rules for walking.

Activity

Walk the route indicated on the map, spending a few minutes at each 'station' and discussing the points of interest. Students note down any of these points of interest.

When you return, students in turn tell of their discoveries at each station, referring to their notes.

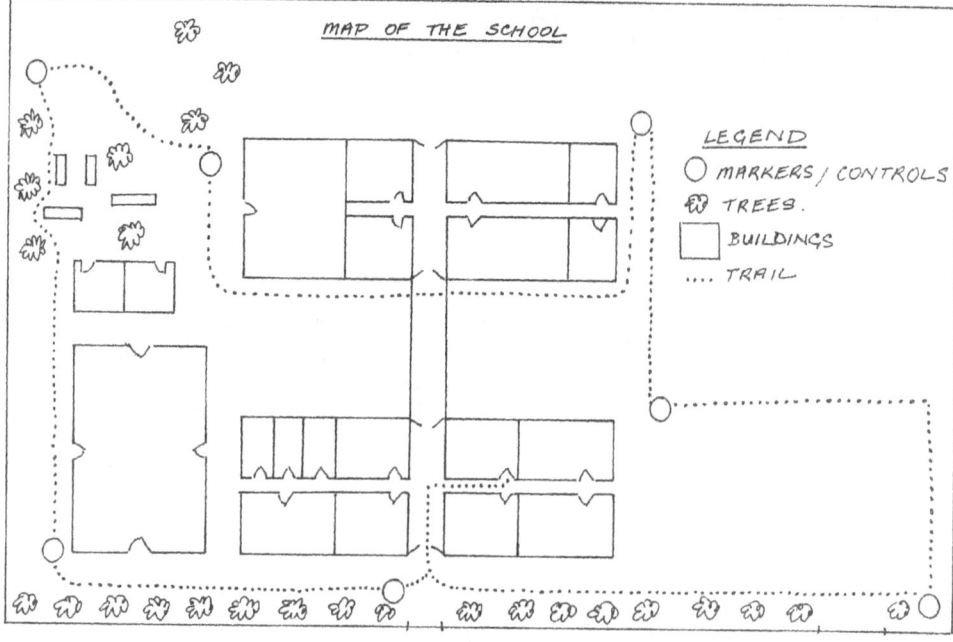

LEVELS 1 AND 2   LESSON 10

SAFETY: RULES IN THE BUSH

Aim
To develop a knowledge of safety rules when in an outdoor environment.

Equipment
- Classroom area
- Adventure playground

Warm Up
One Against Three
Groups of three students numbered 1 to 3 join hands to form triangles. A fourth student tries to touch, in any way possible, the No. 3 person in the triangle. If and when successful, this student takes the place of No. 3 and the game starts again.

Introduction
Discuss the need for an awareness of safety during adventure activities: walking, camping, swimming, studying the environment.

Activity
List adventure activities and write safety rules for each.

Move to the adventure playground. Students move in pairs on a circuit of all pieces of equipment in the adventure playground, taking responsibility for each other's safety.

LEVELS 1 AND 2   LESSON 11

PROBLEM-SOLVING: DEVELOP THINKING

Aim
To develop the student's ability to think through a problem and to solve it.

Equipment
- Marked out squares about 2 m x 2 m
- Length of rope for each pair

Warm Up
Back-to-back Stand
Partners sit back-to-back with knees bent and arms interlocked. Partners stand up by slowly extending legs while backs remain in contact and the body is forced upwards. Then try to go to a sitting position from standing back-to-back.

Introduction
Mark out 2 x 2 m squares about 20 metres apart (or the length of the rope).

Give two participants the end of a 30-metre length rope and ask each of them to stand in one of the squares.

Activity
Students attempt to pull their opponent out of their box.

This game can be extended to 3 or 4 squares by making an appropriately sized piece of rope into a circle larger than the circumference outlined by the squares, and giving the rope to each of the 3-4 participants.

LEVELS 1 AND 2 **LESSON 12**

PROBLEM-SOLVING: ALL ABOARD

Aim
To find out how many students can get on a platform at any one time.

Equipment
- Selected number of gymnasium mats made into a low, flat platform.

Warm Up
Wheelbarrow
While kneeling, one student places their hands on the ground in front of their knees. A partner stands between this student's legs and grasps the ankles or just above the knees. When the legs are raised, the partner walks along on their hands.

Introduction to All Aboard
Explain the rules. In order to be counted as being on the platform each student must have both feet off the ground. All students must be able to hold their pose for at least five seconds.

Activity
Usually an average class can get twelve to fifteen students on the platform, although theoretically, a much larger number is possible. The exercise leads into discussion about team effort, group and individual commitment, leadership, compassion and group problem-solving dynamics.

LEVELS 1 AND 2 — LESSON 13

PROBLEM-SOLVING: POISONOUS JELLY

Aim

To transport an entire group over an area which has been 'smeared with an invisible poisonous jelly substance', using only the following pieces of equipment.

Equipment
- 4 jelly-resistant paper tubes (large, durable and strong cardboard tubes, obtained from any paper company, or anything else that is similar).
- A stout pole measuring about 2 metres and a 10 metre rope (both are resistant to the poison).
- A solid plank about 3 m long, 20 cm wide, 2 cm thick, or a 1 m x 1 m plyboard (6 ply).

Warm Up

City Gates

Two players from each team form arches at wide intervals around the playground. The teams stand in file, in front of their own arches. At a signal, each team runs through its own arch, races around the playground outside the other arches. The game is won by the first team to complete one circuit, pass back through their own arch and to reform in a straight line.

Rules
- The tubes are jelly resistant and may be freely rolled about in this 'viscous poison'.
- The pole is also resistant – the plank or board, however, will dissolve if any part of it 'touches the jelly'.
- Two short lengths of rope mark the area to be crossed. The distance between ropes should be about 10 m. Reduce this distance if needed.
- The 'jelly substance' extends indefinitely within this 10 m band.
- If a participant 'touches the jelly' he or she must quickly return to the starting point and obtain some of the 'super jelly cleaning substance' that allows the participant to begin again.

Alternatives

Many other balance stations can be set up using these versatile tubes. Imagination will give rise to many more. The teacher will need to give a lot of help in this activity.

LEVELS 1 AND 2 **LESSON 14**

PROBLEM-SOLVING: AUDITORY DIRECTION

Aim
To be able to use the sense of hearing to find a destination.

Equipment
- Blindfolds
- Oval
- Bean bags

Warm Up
Circle Catch
A student stands in the centre of a circle (of no more than six students) throwing the bean bag to each student in turn.

Activity
Ask the group (any size) to pair up. Each pair should choose a matching set of words, e.g. salt-pepper, black-white, John-Betty, sock-shoe, etc.

Divide the pairs, and ask each member to walk to opposite ends of a football field, with the instruction that they are each to put on blindfolds at the goal line and, on a signal, try to find their partner by shouting their matching words. All students must only walk (not run) while trying to find their partner.

LEVELS 1 AND 2 **LESSON 15**

PROBLEM-SOLVING: UNNATURAL

Aim

To develop a skill of detecting objects that are out of place in a particular setting.

Equipment
- String for trail
- Any small objects
- Ball

Warm Up

Circle Change Ball

Students spread out into a circle (no more than eight in each circle) with about 1 metre between each student. A ball is passed, (later thrown) around the circle and the player in the centre tries to get it. If the ball is caught, the player takes the place of the player who should have caught it.

Activity

Tie string around trees, buildings, fences, etc. Students follow the string, one at a time, and look for objects which are 'unnatural' to the environment (e.g. pegs, cloth, paper, wool, boxes, candles, etc.) that are on or near the string. Objects can be placed at any level (high or low, etc.). The students count the objects that they see and write them down on a sheet of paper. The winner is the student with the most objects listed.

LEVELS 3 AND 4

No.	Legend	Theme	Subject
1.	♣	Environmental Studies	Trees
2.	♣	Environmental Studies	Grasses
3.	♣	Environmental Studies	Insects
4.	♣	Environmental Studies	Birds
5.		Trailing	Sensory Trail
6.		Trailing	String Trail
7.		Trailing	TV Treasure Hunt
8.		Trailing	Photo Trail
9.		Trailing	Group Trail
10.		Safety	Search Patterns
11.		Mapping	Schoolground
12.		Mapping	Observation Walk
13.		Mapping	Sketch Map Course (easy)
14.		Mapping	Sketch Map Course (harder)
15.		Mapping	Students Develop Courses
16.		Mapping	The Local Environment
17.		Mapping	Observation Trail
18.		Mapping	Route to School
19.	✿	Ropes	Basic Knots
20.	✿	Ropes	Rope Bridges
21.	♀	Problem-solving	Trolley
22.	♀	Problem-solving	Position Change
23.	♀	Problem-solving	Hook Up
24.	♀	Problem-solving	The Four Pointer

LEVELS 3 AND 4   LESSON I

ENVIRONMENTAL STUDIES: TREES

Aim
To classify different types of leaves and bark into tree types.

Equipment
- Leaves and bark from a variety of trees and information
- Books concerning tree classification
- Coloured bands (one band between two students)

Warm Up (optional)
Catch Your Partner's Tail
One partner tucks the coloured band into their skirt or pants for a 'tail', and the other partner chases him or her attempting to steal the tail. Change over.

Activity – Part One
Introduce the idea of 'different types' – different coloured bands, hair colour, the type of clothing worn by different students, also the differences obvious in the environment. What are the different types of nature to be seen in the schoolground (e.g. flowers, plants, trees, etc.)? How can we tell one type of tree from another? Trees can be classified by leaves, flowers, fruit and bark.

Activity – Part Two
Classify leaves by shape, size, texture and smell. (Do not use Oleander leaves in this exercise as they are poisonous.) Compare fruits, seeds and flowers. Compare the various barks.

Classification and comparison activities can be carried out by discussion (pair or small group), a question sheet, a poster presentation, a table arrangement and/or a written summary.

Activity – Part Three
Conduct a grade or class discussion, summarising the ideas and findings discovered during the classification and comparison activities.

LEVELS 3 AND 4   LESSON 2

ENVIRONMENTAL STUDIES: GRASSES

Aim
To discover the services provided by grasses.

Equipment
- A variety of grasses (flowers and seeds) from schoolground or provided by the teacher
- Whistle

Warm Up
Distance Running (5 minutes)
Define an area or pathway to be run around the school perimeter (approximately .5 k in distance). The idea is to run at an even pace until the whistle is blown.

Activity – Part One
Grasses perform several services to soil, insects, animals and man.

Discuss: What are the services (e.g. prevent soil erosion, provide food for animals and humans, protection for insects)? How are they performed?

Activity – Part Two
Search the schoolgrounds for a variety of grasses (flowers and seeds) in season.

Which are weeds? Why?

Revise the types of trees located in the schoolgrounds.

Activity – Part Three
Compare the different types of grasses and trees found in the schoolground.

WALLABY GRASS FLOWERS.

SNOW GRASS.

LEVELS 3 AND 4 **LESSON 3**

ENVIRONMENTAL STUDIES: INSECTS

Aim
To discover the properties of insects.

Equipment
- Reference books and information

Warm Up – Partner Activities

Circle Slap

One partner stands with one hand, palm out, in front of their chest. The other player runs around the partner and slaps the outstretched hand as he or she passes. After five times, change over.

Under and Slap

Partner A stands with feet astride with one hand out, Partner B stands behind A and, on a signal, crawls through A's legs, stands and slaps A's hand then runs behind him or her again and repeats. Change over after five times.

Activity – Part One
What is an insect? How do insects move? Why do insects need to live?

Divide students into small groups to discuss these questions and to formulate some appropriate answers. Appoint a leader, a scribe and a spokesperson for each group. The findings from each group are reported to the grade after a limited time in groups.

Activity – Part Two
Search in places throughout the school suggested by students to find insects (not spiders) – ants, slaters, bees, flies, caterpillars, grasshoppers, crickets, etc.

Activity – Part Three
As a class, compare the groups' findings about any ideas or discoveries made during the outside 'search'.

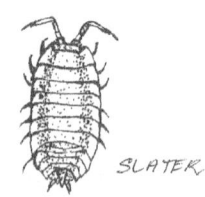

LEVELS 3 AND 4 — LESSON 4

ENVIRONMENTAL STUDIES: BIRDS

Aim
To categorise different birds into a number of types and behaviours.

Equipment
- Reference books and information
- 5 hoops and 12 bean bags

Warm Up
Bean Bag Scramble
Make up four teams of equal numbers and number each player. When a number is called, that player from each team races to take one bean bag at a time and place it in in their own hoop. When all bean bags are taken, he or she may rob another hoop, taking one bean bag at a time. The first team to obtain four bean bags wins a point. Repeat the game until all players have had a turn.

Activity – Part One
Sit outside very still (e.g. on the oval, on a grassed area) and listen to the sounds of the environment. What sounds can be heard? Some are unnatural sounds (e.g. traffic, machinery, etc.) and others are natural (e.g. wind, dogs, birds).

Listen in particular to the bird noises. Are they all the same? How can different birds be recognised?

Birds can be recognised by sight, colour, size, shape, sound, behaviour, nesting, feeding, mating.

Activity – Part Two
Move around the schoolgrounds or local environment (e.g. park, streets) and list the birds that are seen and the behaviour they exhibit.

Where were they sighted? What were they doing?

Activity – Part Three
Several students may volunteer, or be selected, to characterise, imitate or describe a type of bird and its behaviour for other students to guess what bird it is.

LEVELS 3 AND 4　　　　　　　　　　　　　　　　LESSON 5

TRAILING: SENSORY TRAIL

Aim

To recognise trees, grasses, insects and birds.

Equipment
- Ball of string
- Examples of trees (bark, leaves) weeds, insects and birds (photos/pictures)
- Blindfolds enough for half the group
- 1 rope per student

Warm Up

Skipping Activities

Have the students skip on the spot with the rope in various directions with frequent changes: knees high, taking small steps, change to long bounding skips.

Activity – Part One

Preparation. Before the lesson, set up the string trail by wrapping around posts, seats, trees, etc. Select a number of locations on the trail to set up various stations at which each pair of students will stop.

In pairs, blindfold one partner while the 'seeing' partner acts as a guide, ensuring that the 'blindfolded' student maintains contact with the string. Half-way along the trail students exchange blindfolds and roles.

Activity – Part Two

At each location, the blindfolded student attempts to describe, recognise or guess the example by feeling or smelling it. If a photo/picture card is at the location, the 'seeing' partner describes or reads the information to their partner. Find out how many examples your partner can recognise.

Activity – Part Three

Allow the students to offer their opinions concerning how they felt during the blindfold activities.

LEVELS 3 AND 4 **LESSON 6**

TRAILING: STRING TRAIL

Aim
To learn to discriminate between environmental objects.

Equipment
- A ball of string
- Approximately 25 'unnatural' objects (e.g. pegs, cloth, blocks, key ring, cans, ruler, etc.)

Warm Up
Chain Tag
Two players are chosen as 'it'. They join hands and chase other players who, when tagged, join hands with 'it'. Only the players at each end of the 'it' chain are allowed to tag.

Activity – Part One
Preparation. Prior to the lesson, select a small area which has a number of trees, seats and equipment to which the string may be tied. At various intervals along or near the string, tie or place different 'unnatural' objects.

Divide the students into two groups. Each group begins at either end of the string trail.

Explain that the aim of this trail is to use one's sight effectively to locate and count environmental objects.

Activity – Part Two
As the students walk individually along the trail, each attempts to locate by sight (without touching the string or any objects or calling out what they have found) and count the number of objects discovered.

Activity – Part Three
With the teacher, all the students walk along the trail following the string and locating each environmental object.

LEVELS 3 AND 4 **LESSON 7**

TRAILING:
TV TREASURE HUNT

Aim
To locate a number of hidden cards in a particular area.

Equipment
- 15 cards (approximately 30 cm × 6 cm) with various television programs written on them
- Pen and pad for each pair

Warm Up
Distance Running (5 minutes)
Define an area or pathway to be run around the school perimeter (approximately 0.5 k distance). The idea is to run at an even pace until the whistle is blown.

Activity – Part One
Preparation. Before the lesson, select a particular area around the school (e.g. near buildings, breezeway) to fix the TV treasure hunt cards to walls, door, poles, etc.

Explain to the students that they must find fifteen cards which are hidden in a particular area.

Activity – Part Two
In pairs, the students attempt to locate the cards and write down the answers (TV programs) from each card. When each card is found do not let the students call out, but ask them to be very secretive about its location.

The first pair to return to the teacher with all fifteen correctly answered TV program questions, are the winners.

LEVELS 3 AND 4 **LESSON 8**

TRAILING:
PHOTO TRAIL

Aim

To recognise each photo presented and to describe the location in the schoolground.

Equipment
- A series of school photographs (approximately 15) depicting different points around the school (various perspectives)
- 2 witch's hat markers per team

Warm Up

Over Legs Relay

Have approximately six students in a team. No. 1 stands up and runs over the legs of their team up to and around a witch's hat, and then back down over the legs, around another witch's hat and back to their place, tapping No.2 who continues the game.

Activity – Part One

Explain the idea of the game. The winner is the first student to recognise each photo and describe its exact location; then all progress to that location and the next photo is shown and so on.

Activity – Part Two

Take the students to a neutral position and show them the first photo. The first student to recognise the photo and describe where it is in the school is awarded a point. The students all run to that location and another photo is shown. Continue in this way to last photo.

Activity – Part Three

Ask the students to repeat the order in which each photo was presented (e.g. Photo No. 1 was … Photo No. 2 … etc.).

LEVELS 3 AND 4   LESSON 9

TRAILING: GROUP TRAIL

Aim

To devise a number of trails in groups.

Equipment

- A quantity of cards of different colours

Warm Up

Jumping Activities

Jump on the spot. Try jumping for height; rhythmic jumping feet apart, together, to the side, forwards, backwards; jump making shapes in the air, touching various body parts; standing broad-jump; count the number of jumps taken to reach a nominated spot.

Activity – Part One

Divide the students into groups of approximately four to five. Select a theme such as numbers, words, signs or symbols. Write the subject on ten cards.

Each group has different coloured cards. The group may choose to hide each card in a treasure-hunt style, or to link each card with drawn arrows on the cards, or chalk arrows on the ground.

Activity – Part Two

Each group quickly lays its trail of cards in different areas around the school. When finished, pair the students and have them track other trails. The answers from each card are recorded. A check that each pair has completed the course is enabled by a check of the codes recorded from each card (control) visited.

Activity – Part Three

Discuss the different types of trails set in the various areas.

What kinds of places were selected to hide the cards? Were the cards difficult to find? What trail did you enjoy tracking? Why?

LEVELS 3 AND 4 **LESSON 10**

SAFETY: SEARCH PATTERNS

Aim
To simulate a search for two 'lost' people.

Equipment
- 1 small ball between 3 students

Warm Up
One Against Three
Three students join hands. One other student is the tagger. By dodging and moving around, the group of three try to prevent No. 1 from touching No. 4.

Activity – Part One
By introducing the fact that people are lost in unfamiliar and seemingly familiar environments every year, ask the students, 'What can we do if we get lost?'. Some of the responses could be:
In a 'lost' situation I would:
- Call out 'help'
- Remain in the one position,
- Etc.

Activity – Part Two
Two students are selected as the 'lost' people and leave to find a place to hide in the schoolground. The rest of the students comprise the rescue group and must work out how they will find the 'lost' people.
Will the rescuers
- Divide into small groups or stay together?
- Need any rescue equipment?
- Need to know the area beforehand?
- Etc.

Activity – Part Three
Question the students about their methods of rescue.

Did they make effective decisions or could they have been improved? How did the 'lost' people feel?

Ask the students: What would it be like if you were really lost in bushland by yourself?

LEVELS 3 AND 4 — LESSON 11

MAPPING: SCHOOLGROUND

Aim

To recognise different features on a map of the school.

Equipment
- Multiple copies of a school map (1 per student)
- Coloured bands (1 per student)

Warm Up (optional)

Scarecrow Team Tag

Two teams. The 'banded' team tries to tag the 'unbanded' team. On a signal, the 'unbanded' team tags the 'banded' team. Define the tag area.

Activity – Part One

Discuss what kinds of maps are available. The responses could include street maps and directories, maps of different suburbs and areas, aerial photograph maps, maps of different countries, a world map, etc.

Activity – Part Two

Distribute duplicated maps of the school to the students. Question the students about where particular rooms and grades are, what teacher belongs to which room, which direction does the front of the school face, etc.

Emphasise the need for a key or legend so that particular areas (such as the art room, the library, the music rooms, grade rooms, the hall or multipurpose rooms, the staffroom, the oval, the gardens, etc.) can be easily and quickly recognised.

Activity – Part Three

Compare the types of features and the key on the school map with other types of maps.

LEVELS 3 AND 4
LESSON 12

MAPPING: OBSERVATION WALK

Aim
To be able to relate map features to specific areas in the school.

Equipment
- Sketch maps used in Lesson 11

Warm Up
Leapfrog
Leapfrog over partner several times.

Activity – Part One
Distribute maps. Select a pathway to be taken on a walk round the school. This pathway is marked by a trail (see Lesson 9). Explain the pathway to the students.

Activity – Part Two
As the students follow the trail, they will come upon markers. The positions of all fifteen markers have to be recorded by each student on each individual map.

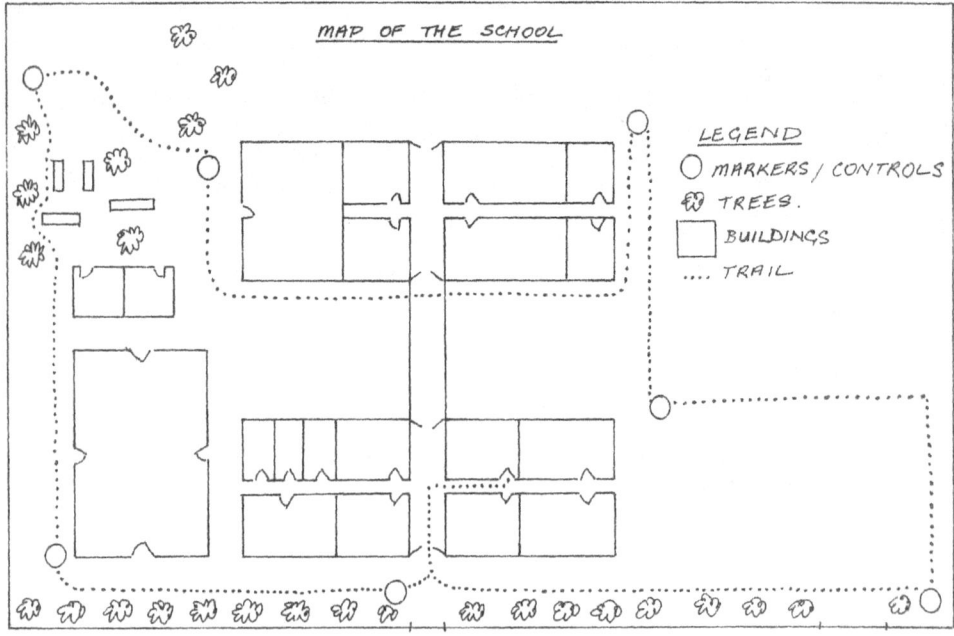

LEVELS 3 AND 4 LESSON 13

MAPPING: SKETCH MAP COURSE (EASY)

Aim

To be able to use a map to locate specific points in the school ground.

Equipment

- Duplicated multiple copies of a map of the school, (1 map per student) with 10 controls (navigation points) circled on map
- 10 navigation cards (all one colour – e.g. green) with one letter written on each which, when all the cards are put together, will make a word (e.g. navigation)
- Note pads (1 for each student)

Warm Up

Train Relay (5 to 6 students in a team)
Standing in relay formation, the engine (first person) runs from line A to line B and back to pick up the next carriage. Then both engine and carriage repeat the run, picking up successive carriages.

Activity – Part One

Preparation. Prior to the lesson, the ten navigation cards are taped in the positions (at various heights) as designated by the course No. 1 map of the school.

Explain the concept of navigation in outdoor activities. In this course, the students (in pairs) must locate each circled point on the map somewhere in the schoolgrounds. Within each circle a coloured navigation card will be found at any height. On their pads, each pair writes down the letter written on each card.

Activity – Part Two

Set pairs off on the navigation trail (with a thirty second break between each pair). Emphasise that they need to carefully study the points located on the map, find the cards quickly, and to run between each point to see who can get back to the start the quickest.

Activity – Part Three

Check the student's written result (i.e. navigation) and the time taken to find all the letters around the school.

LEVELS 3 AND 4　　　　　　　　　　　　　　　　LESSON 14

MAPPING: SKETCH MAP COURSE (HARDER)

Aim
To be able to use a map to locate specific points in the schoolground.

Equipment
- Duplicated copies of a school map (1 map per student) with 10 different points circled on the map (controls)
- 10 navigation cards (all one colour, e.g. blue) with a word written on each card e.g. treasure, building, trail, mapping, etc.
- Note pads (1 for each student)

Warm Up
Hopping Activities
Hop on one foot. Change to the other – move around the area; hop to spell out names in giant letters; hop on one foot and place the other leg in various positions (e.g. out in front, tucked up behind, swinging leg, etc.); try a hopping race with a partner.

Activity – Part One
Preparation. Prior to the lesson, the ten navigation cards are taped in the positions (at various heights) as designated by the course No. 2 map.

Explain the concept of navigation in outdoor activities. In this course, the students (in pairs) must locate each circled point on the map somewhere in the schoolgrounds. Within each circle a coloured navigation card (e.g. blue) will be found at any height. On your pad write down the word written on each card.

Activity – Part Two
Start pairs off on the navigation trail (with a thirty second break between each pair). Emphasise that they need to carefully study the points located on the map, find the cards quickly, and to run between each point to see who can get back to the start the quickest.
* This course can be more difficult than that of Lesson 13.

Activity – Part Three
Check the student's written result (i.e. navigation) and the time taken to find all the letters round the school.

LEVELS 3 AND 4 — LESSON 15

MAPPING: STUDENTS DEVELOP COURSES

Aim
To plan and prepare navigation trail.

Equipment
- A number of coloured cards to be used as markers
- Tape and pens
- Duplicated maps of school
- Whistle
- Note pads (1 for each student)

Warm Up
Distance Running (5 minutes)
Define an area or pathway to be run along (e.g. along the school perimeter, oval, etc.). The idea is to run each lap at an even pace until the whistle is blown, then the first student back to the start is the winner.

Activity – Part One
Explain how to plan the navigation trail by referring to the map of the school and selecting ten stations or points to be circled. Prepare the ten cards or markers by placing a word, a letter, a number, a sign or a symbol on each.

Divide the students into groups quickly so that the planning and preparation can quickly take place.

Activity – Part Two
Each group quickly tapes the ten marker cards at the specific points located on the group map of the school.

When completed, the groups exchange maps so that a new trail can be followed around the school. The codes, words or messages written on the cards should be copied down by each group.

Activity – Part Three
Collect all ten marker cards from each group around the school and compare the planning and preparation of each group.

LEVELS 3 AND 4   **LESSON 16**

MAPPING:
THE LOCAL ENVIRONMENT

Aim

To recognise features on a map of the local area.

Equipment

- Duplicated copies of a map of the local area

Warm Up (optional)

Hospital Tag

A player, when touched, must hold the part of the body where he or she was touched and, with this handicap, chase the others.

Activity – Part One

Distribute the duplicated maps of the local area and allow time for the students to familiarise themselves with the streets and features of the map. Ask the students to find where they live on the map and then trace the route they take to and from school each day. Draw and colour in a small square to represent each student's house and then lightly colour in the streets that the students walk along on their way to school.

Review the concept of a legend. Encourage the students to suggest various features (on or that can be added to the map) that can belong to a legend e.g. shops, railway station, schools, etc. Colour code these features and add them to the legend.

Activity – Part Two

Discuss the different routes or trails that could be taken along streets close to the school.

After identifying the route that will be taken (for the following lesson) the students colour it in on the map.

Activity – Part Three

Collect the maps for use in the next session.

LEVELS 3 AND 4 *LESSON 17*

MAPPING: OBSERVATION TRAIL

Aim
To follow a prescribed route from a map.

Equipment
Maps from Lesson 16

Warm Up
Partner Activity – Push/Pull Tug-of-War
Partners face each other, squatting down with arms extended and hands clasped. Each attempt to push or pull (on a signal) the other across an imaginary line between them.

Activity – Part One
Quickly revise the route selected to be taken along the observation trail. Highlight the type of environmental aspects that one might expect to see along the way.

Activity – Part Two
During the walk around the local neighbourhood streets, see how many different types of environmental examples: trees, plants, insects, birds – are within the area.

Activity – Part Three
Briefly discuss some of the interesting observations made during the walk.

LEVELS 3 AND 4 **LESSON 18**

MAPPING: ROUTE TO SCHOOL

Aim
To reproduce a route to school as a sketch map.

Equipment
- Duplicated maps of local area
- Plain paper for sketching
- Coloured pencils

Warm Up (optional)
Circle Chase
Form a large circle and number players in fours. When a number (1 to 4) is called, the players so numbered run around the outside of the circle to the right and return to their places. Before reaching their place, players aim to tag the runner ahead. Any player tagged is eliminated.

Activity – Part One
Revise the features on the local map as recognised by the legend. A map identification symbol or code game may be an appropriate and enjoyable method of revision.

Revision questions may include:
What is the name of this code? Who can describe what a creek or river may look like on a map? What colour would a park or reserve on a map most likely be?

Activity – Part Two
As the students have previously identified their own address and the way they come to school, question the students how a copy of that particular route may be taken from the map.

Students then reproduce their route to school as a sketch map, making sure that directions are accurate.

Activity – Part Three
Compare the different sketch maps made by the students of their route to school.

LEVELS 3 AND 4 LESSON 19

ROPES: BASIC KNOTS

Aim
To learn to tie some basic knots that can be used in survival situations.

Equipment
- Lengths of cord (sisal or nylon are best)
- Some strong sticks

Warm Up (optional)
Running Activities
Try free running in all directions (forwards, backwards, sideways), over different levels (high, low); dodging in, out and around equipment. Place the right hand on the ground and run around in a clockwise direction, repeat in an anticlockwise direction and with the left hand. Try shadowing – imitate partners varying leg and arm actions.

Activity – Part One
Explain to the students that there are many uses for some basic knots that can be used in survival situations.

Activity – Part Two
Demonstrate and describe the following easier knots:
- Reef knot
- Bowline
- Round turn and two half hitches
- Clove hitch

In pairs, the students attempt to copy and practise some of these knots.

Activity – Part Three
Discuss the care of ropes:
- Rough surfaces and sharp edges wear the fibres of the rope and so reduce its strength.
- Internal wear is caused by dirt and grit working its way beneath the fibres.
- Before storing, ropes should be clean and dry, then hung loosely in coils. Rot and mildew rapidly destroy rope fibres.

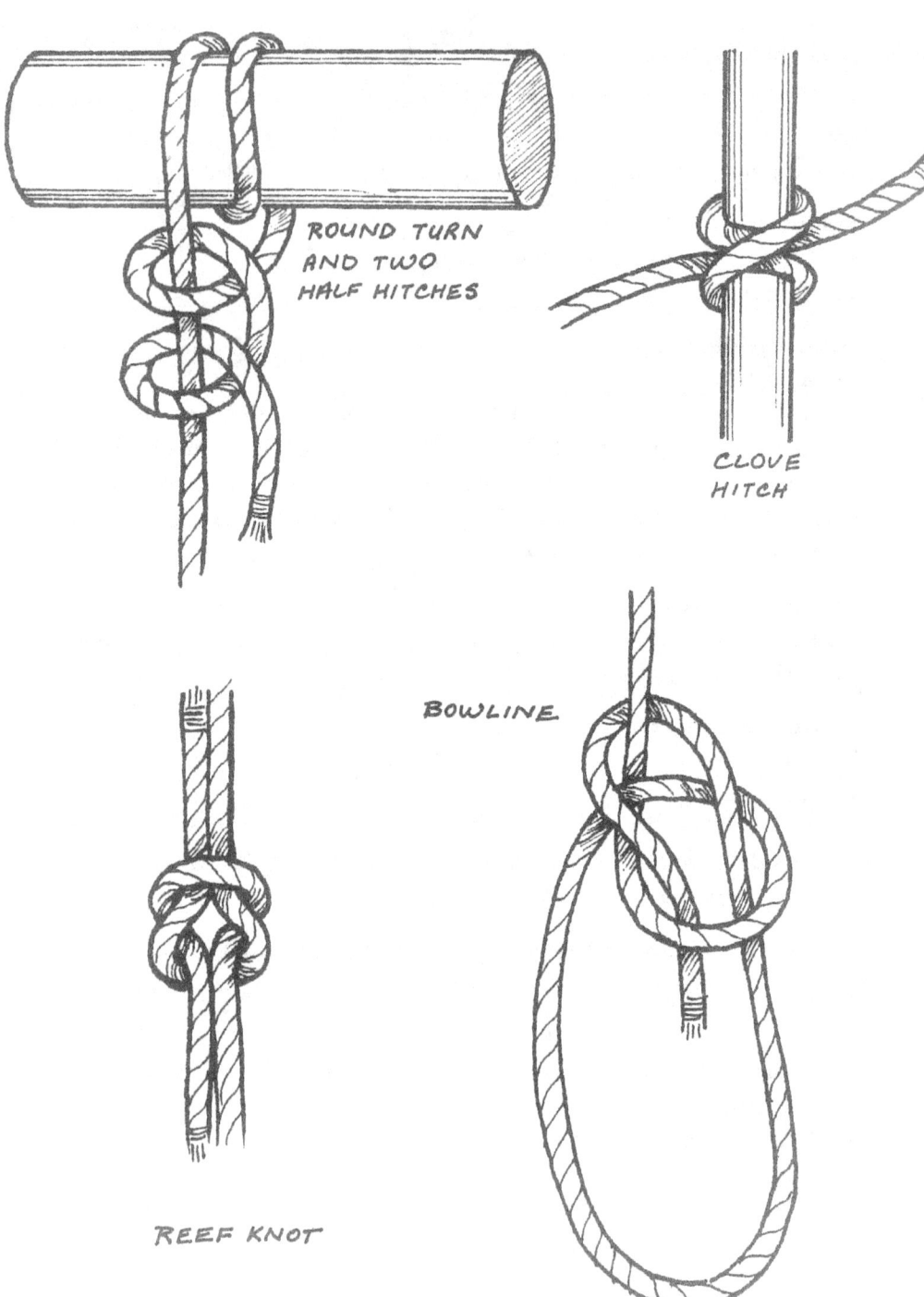

LEVELS 3 AND 4 **LESSON 20**

ROPES:
ROPE BRIDGES

Aim
To use various basic knots to make a rope construction.

Equipment
- Lengths of cord, string
- Some strong sticks, small twigs or icy-pole sticks

Warm Up (optional)
Squirrel in a Tree
Players form into groups of three. Two hold hands (tree) with the third player (squirrel) in the middle. Odd players become spare squirrels. On 'change', squirrels skip around area until 'home' is called and all squirrels run to a tree (group of two). Always one or two squirrels are left over.

Activity – Part One
Discuss the types of constructions which are possible to make quickly and which are extremely useful in a survival situation. Revise the basic knots learned in Lesson 19.

Activity – Part Two
In the classroom in small groups or pairs, students may choose to make either a large or small construction:

Large or small
- Rope
- Ladder
- Scramble net
- Climbing ropes

Small
- Burmese bridge
- Horizontal ladder
- Two-line bridge

Activity – Part Three
Observe the different constructions made by each group or pair.

LEVELS 3 AND 4   LESSON 21

PROBLEM-SOLVING: TROLLEY

Aim
To move small groups of people over a 'poisoned jelly area' as efficiently as possible.

Equipment
- Planks of wood (approximately 30 cm by 2.5 m)
- Lengths of rope, cord

Warm Up
Top and Bottom Relay (5 to 6 students per group)
On the command of 'top', the head of the file stands still while team members run around him or her and back to their places. On the command 'bottom', the team members run around the bottom person.

Activity – Part One
Explain the object of the situation, which is:

> 'As efficiently as possible, move your group over the 'poisoned jelly area' utilizing the given equipment (two planks of wood) per group and two lengths of cord or rope per student), without anyone in the group touching the 'noxious substance' with any part of their body (including clothes, shoes, etc.).'

Rules: If someone falls off the trolley, add a time penalty for each time a member of the crew touches the ground.

Activity – Part Two
Trying to manoeuvre the 'trolley' around or over an obstacle adds a different dimension to the problem as an extra challenge to fast movers.

Activity – Part Three
Discuss and compare the methods used by each crew to approach the problem.

LEVELS 3 AND 4 *LESSON 22*

PROBLEM-SOLVING: POSITION CHANGE

Aim

To successfully change positions on a balance beam or bench.

Equipment
- A balance beam or bench per group
- Whistle

Warm Up

Distance Running

Define an area or pathway to be run along (e.g. along the school perimeter, oval, etc.). The idea is to run each lap at an even pace until the whistle is blown, then the first student back to the start is the winner.

Activity – Part One

By explaining the aim of 'position change', i.e. the students in each group must pass each other to get to the other end of the beam without falling off, the need to cooperate and communicate with each other will be reinforced.

In groups of approximately five to six students (depending on the length of the beam), two or three students try to get to the other end of the beam, while the rest of the students endeavour to pass them to get to the opposite end.

Activity – Part Two

To make this activity a little harder, one student from each group:
- Can be selected to pass a number of other students on the beam;
- Tries to get to the other end of the beam as quickly as possible.

Activity – Part Three

Question the students as to how they felt during the activity.

LEVELS 3 AND 4 — LESSON 23

PROBLEM-SOLVING: HOOK UP

Aim
To attempt to 'hook up' an object and take it from location to location without directly touching it.

Equipment
- 2 long ropes, coathangers (used as hooks) and a handled bucket (per group)
- A variety of objects (e.g. boxes, chairs, hoops, etc, for a greater challenge)
- 1 bean bag per two students

Warm Up
Partner Activity – Bean Bag Grab
Partners line up opposite each other on either side of an area which has the bean bag in the middle. On the signal, each partner attempts to grab the bean bag first. Different starting positions may be used (e.g. sitting, lying on front/back, balancing, etc.).

Activity – Part One
Explain the object of the problem and divide the students into groups of four. Each group has two long pieces of rope or cord which are joined/knotted together at the middle to form a cross. At the centre of the ropes attach a coathanger hook.

In groups of four (each group member holds one end of the tied rope) all work together (verbalising and moving) to attempt to pick up a handled bucket from point A and navigate a pathway to a point B, without dropping the bucket or letting it touch the ground.

Activity – Part Two
Alternatively, to make the above situation more challenging, the bucket may be filled with water and/or various objects (e.g. boxes, seats, hoops) must be climbed over or navigated around, under or through during the activity.

Activity – Part Three
Have the students watch the methods used by other groups in attempting to negotiate the bucket around the area.

LEVELS 3 AND 4 **LESSON 24**

PROBLEM-SOLVING: THE FOUR POINTER

Aim
To attempt to get a group of students across a wide area, using only four points of simultaneous contact with the ground.

Warm Up
Circle Change
Make two circles (one inside the other) facing the centre. Players in the outside circle put their hands on the shoulders of those in the inside circle. Everyone in the inner circle joins hands. All sides skip clockwise or anticlockwise. On the command 'change one (two or three) places' those in the outside group let go of the shoulders of those in front, and run (faster) in the same direction as the circles are moving to reach the shoulders of the next person in the inner circle.

Activity – Part One
Explain the object of this problem-solving situation, i.e. each group must attempt to get all members of its group (eight) across a wide area (approximately ten to fifteen metres), using only four points of simultaneous contact with the ground. (e.g. foot, knee, hand, etc.).

Rules
1. All eight students must start at the marked starting line and end at the finish line.
2. No props (logs, ropes) may be used.
3. All eight students in each group must be in contact with each other as they progress across the area.

Activity – Part Two
Have all groups make the attempt simultaneously so that they will discover solutions independently.

Activity – Part Three
Compare the various methods used by each of the groups during the crossing.

LEVEL 5

No.	Legend	Theme	Subject
1.	♣	Environmental Studies	Environmental Search
2.	♣	Environmental Studies	Environmental Search
3.	♣	Environmental Studies	Classification
4.	♣	Environmental Studies	Classification
5.	♣	Environmental Studies	Nature Trail
6.	♣	Environmental Studies	Nature Trail
7.	🗺	Mapping	Plan
8.	🗺	Mapping	School Map
9.	🗺	Mapping	Direction
10.	🗺	Mapping	Representations
11.	🗺	Mapping	Colour in Maps
12.	🗺	Mapping	Observation Trail
13.	🗺	Mapping	Drawing a Trail
14.	🗺	Mapping	Legend
15.	✹	Navigation	Compass Use (introduction)
16.	✹	Navigation	Compass Use
17.	✹	Navigation	Compass Use
18.	✹	Navigation	Revision
19.	✹	Navigation	Compass Walk
20.	✹	Navigation	Compass Points
21.	✿	Ropes	Knots
22.	✿	Ropes	Rope Bridges
23.	△	Bushcraft	Fire Lighting
24.	△	Bushcraft	Campfire
25.	△	Bushcraft	Problem-solving in Fire Lighting

LEVEL 5   **LESSON 1**

ENVIRONMENTAL STUDIES: ENVIRONMENTAL SEARCH

Aim
To develop skills of observation and searching.

Equipment
- Classification sheets
- Clear tape

Activity
The classification sheet contains twelve concepts, such as rough, pointed, shiny, smelly, etc. The task is for the students to find as many of the twelve objects as possible, sticking the objects on the sheet in the respective spaces.

The objects should be found in the schoolground and should be natural objects – not manufactured by man. It is preferable that each object be made of a different substance.

This is the initial type of classification:

LEVEL 5 LESSON 2

ENVIRONMENTAL STUDIES: ENVIRONMENTAL SEARCH

Aim
To encourage skills of observation in the environment.

Equipment
- Alphabetical sheets
- Clear tape

Activity
The students fill in the sheets using objects found in the school yard, matching the first letter of the object with that on the sheet.

These objects may be manufactured or natural, or both. However, it is preferable if they are natural.

Emphasis is placed on originality, and in matching some of the more difficult letters, give encouragement to those who use initiative: e.g.
A - Acacia leaf
B - Berry
C - Clover
D - Dirt

At the end of a prearranged period of time, the student with the most letters completed is the winner.

A ACACIA	B BLACKBERRY	C CLOVER	D DIRT	E	F
G GUM FLOWER	H HAIR	I	J	K	L
M	N	O	P	Q	R

LEVEL 5　　　　　　　　　　　　　　LESSON 3

ENVIRONMENTAL STUDIES: CLASSIFICATION

Aim

To encourage and aid methods of classification.

Equipment
- Clip board
- Paper
- Pencil
- Classification sheets

Activity

Have the students, in a group with the teacher, walk around the streets adjacent to the school.

Groups of students will predetermine certain categories of objects that are similar.

Probably five or six categories may be determined. Examples of categories could be lists of objects that are:
- Manufactured
- Natural (original trees or land forms)
- Planted by people
- Below 1 metre in height
- As tall as a light-pole
- In need of repair
- Of the same colour.

At school, collate these lists and write them down on charts classifying them into groups: Manufactured, New, Light Colour, Natural, Old, Dark Colour.

LEVEL 5　　　　　　　　　　　　　　　　　　　　　　　LESSON 4

ENVIRONMENTAL STUDIES: CLASSIFICATION

Aim

To further classify objects collected from Lesson 3.

Equipment

- Lists made up in Lesson 3

Activity

Ask the students to look at the lists made up in Lesson 3, and endeavour to make new categories within these lists, i.e. 'classes within each classification', e.g.

- Within 'manufactured' there may be timber objects or metal objects;
- Within 'natural' there may be tall or short trees;
- Within 'planted' there may be flowering or non-flowering;
- Etc.

These lists may then be reconstructed to incorporate subclasses, to further enhance the concept of classification, and to demonstrate that classification may take many directions.

MAN MADE		NEW		LIGHT COLOUR	
PUBLIC PROPERTY	PRIVATELY OWNED	FINISHED	UNFINISHED	SINGLE COLOUR	MULTIPLE COLOUR
PHONE BOX	FENCE	PARK BENCH	HOUSE FRAME	YELLOW ROSE	VARIGATED LEAF
FIRE HYDRANT	MAIL BOX				

NATURAL		OLD		DARK COLOUR	
TALL	SHORT	HARD	SOFT	SHINY	DULL
GHOST GUM	GRASS	ROCKS	FALLEN AUTUMN LEAVES	BLACK CAR	DIRT
				COCKROACH	

LEVEL 5   **LESSON 5**

ENVIRONMENTAL STUDIES: NATURE TRAIL

Aim

To introduce, through a nature trail, positive elements of environmental studies.

Equipment
- Nature trail sheets
- Pencil

Activity

This type of trail can be developed anywhere around the school, particularly where the school has plants in the grounds.

The students are given explicit instructions about where to find an object. This type of trail tries to develop the skills of following simple instructions with information about each point, when this point is found.

There should be at least eight to twelve points, and each point should be fairly easy to find.

The set of information about each point should be kept for future reference. e.g.
- CONTROL ONE is located six steps inside front gate.
- CONTROL TWO is located in the area on the ground next to the monkey bars.

LEVEL 5　　　　　　　　　　　　　　　　　　LESSON 6

ENVIRONMENTAL STUDIES: NATURE TRAIL

Aim

To further enhance the nature trail concept, but with emphasis on the environmental information.

Equipment
- Nature trail sheets
- Numbered cards

Activity

The purpose of this trail is to provide the students with specific clues and information about natural objects (or if the schoolground does not possess sufficient natural features, then any features will suffice), in the schoolground. Each of the objects described is assigned a letter of the alphabet. This is a code which is recorded and later used to check that each object has been visited.

The students look at the clues they are given and, through observation, match up the clue with the respective letter, e.g.
- It has long green leaves.
- It has seed pods, about the size of a pea.
- At this time of the year, it has red flowers that are round, and with many little spikes.
- The tree is very tall.

ANSWER: RED FLOWERING GUM

The name of the respective plant or feature is also matched with the assigned letter. This then provides a set of names and descriptions of sets of natural features (particularly plants) around the school.

LEVEL 5   LESSON 7

MAPPING: PLAN

Aim
To introduce the concept of mapping as a 'bird's eye view'.

Equipment
- Paper
- Pencil
- Ruler

Activity
At this stage, scale will not be discussed to any great depth, but it should be pointed out that, if an object is small, it should be represented that way, and if the same object is bigger than another, it would be shown that way as well.

The students should be aware of relative distances, i.e. approximate distances of features in relation to others.

This first exercise is to get the students to simply draw their classroom, with the roof lifted off, as though they were a bird. They should draw the furniture, where they sit, where their friends sit, where their teacher sits, etc. They should put an arrow towards the nearest street, and an arrow pointing to the side of the school where the sun is shining at lunchtime.

Colour this map with similar features the same colour. Ensure a legend is included.

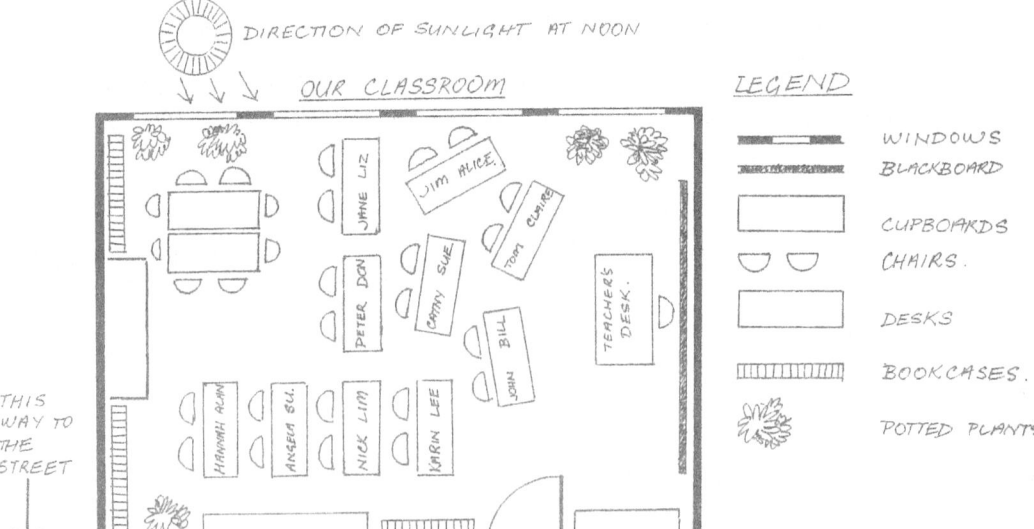

LEVEL 5   LESSON 8

MAPPING: SCHOOL MAP

Aim

To develop further concepts in maps.

Equipment

- Paper
- Pencil
- Ruler

Activity

As in Lesson 7, it is not necessary to emphasise scale, but merely to encourage the students to appreciate differences in size and special relations of respective features.

Have the students attempt to draw a map of the school, showing relative positions of buildings to play areas, playground equipment, etc.

They should especially show their classrooms, the streets around the school, and their names. Any notable features should be labelled, and similar features coloured the same. Again, coloured features should be labelled at the side, to distinguish them.

As in Lesson 7, the direction of the sun at lunchtime should be included.

LEVEL 5   LESSON 9

MAPPING: DIRECTION

Aim

To develop an ability to determine and describe directions.

Equipment

- Paper
- Pencil

Activity

This lesson is simply one of description, to describe as accurately as possible the direction the students take to get from school to their homes.

Begin by having them name the street adjacent to the school, and then which direction from the school gate they take when they leave. They must use left or right and, where possible, street names, e.g. turn right at Waratah Street. While continuing along a particular street, they should note if they cross another street and, if possible, name it.

After the description has been written, have the students draw their description – simple one-line maps are adequate. Ensure that their drawings match their descriptions.

Keep these drawings for the next lesson.

Introduce the four cardinal directions – North, East, South and West.

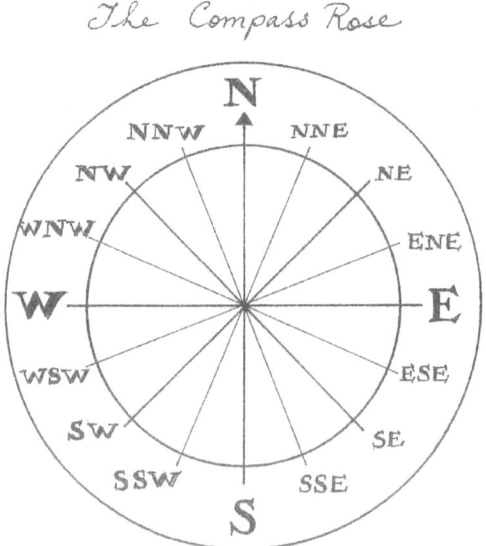

The Compass Rose

LEVEL 5   LESSON 10

MAPPING: REPRESENTATIONS

Aim

To look at and appreciate different representations of the same area.

Equipment
- Sketch map from Lesson 8
- Street directory
- Aerial photograph of the area (try Google maps)

Activity

The main emphasis in this lesson is to compare differences in the same areas of land as they are represented in different maps and photos.

The first task is to compare the student's sketch maps with a street directory to see the differences between the two.

The second is to look for these features present on both the street directory and on an aerial photograph and again compare the differences, particularly such things as the school, the student's homes, the shopping centre, railway lines, main roads, etc.

LEVEL 5   LESSON 11

MAPPING: COLOUR IN MAPS

Aim

To learn some of the concepts of coloured representation on maps.

Equipment
- Street directory
- Any Army survey maps
- Maps of the state

Activity

By comparing two or three types of maps the students determine what colours are used for the same objects or physical features.

If the students have kept their sketch maps they should refer to these and compare the colours they used to those used on the printed maps.

List those features that are similarly represented and show the colours. From this exercise, develop a basic legend which can be used on all maps.

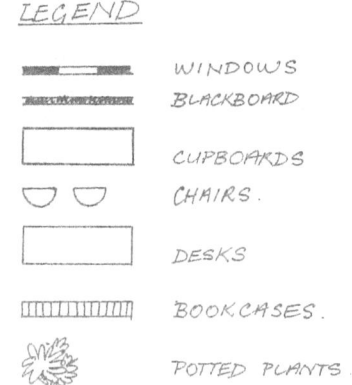

LEVEL 5 *LESSON 12*

MAPPING: OBSERVATION TRAIL

Aim

To aid the development of mapping skills in terms of relating physical features to the map.

Equipment
- Observation trail
- Pencil
- Clip board
- Copies of a street directory page of the school district

Activity

The prerequisite for this lesson is the preparation of an observation of the district surrounding the school. Any outstanding features of the area should be included in the trail, which should include ten to twelve items.

The students are required to find where those features are on a street map, i.e. they should estimate the locations.

Features that may be included are:
- Large tree
- Post office
- Letter box
- Fire hydrant
- Phone box
- Traffic lights
- Football ground
- Supermarket
- School
- Police station.

LEVEL 5　　　　　　　　　　　　　　　　　　　　　　　　　　　**LESSON 13**

MAPPING: DRAWING A TRAIL

Aim

As for Lesson 12: to augment the ability to transpose physical features to a map.

Equipment
- Map of schoolground
- Pencil

Activity

Using the observation trail that the students have already completed, locate the points on the trail as accurately as possible on the map of the schoolground. This should include the name of the feature. Perhaps several of these nature trails, after being plotted on the map, could provide a ready reference of environmental 'objects' in the schoolground, e.g. this map could be a ready locational source of nature plants, etc.

Then, similarly to classifications, like objects could be plotted in like colours or markings, providing further enhancement of the concept of 'legend'.

LEVEL 5 LESSON 14

MAPPING: LEGEND

Aim
To make the students fully aware and be able to understand the concept of mapping and, in particular that of 'legend'.

Equipment
- Army survey maps
- Street directory
- Paper
- Coloured pencils
- Felt-tipped pens

Activity
By using the maps and the street directories, have the students determine what are the most common symbols and what they represent.

These responses should then be put on charts which the students make and be displayed round their classroom.

From the objects that they previously selected from the neighbourhood and located on their maps, the students should mutually agree on symbols that could be used, e.g.
- Large tree
- Fire hydrant
- Phone box
- Letter box, etc.

These may also be put on a chart and displayed.

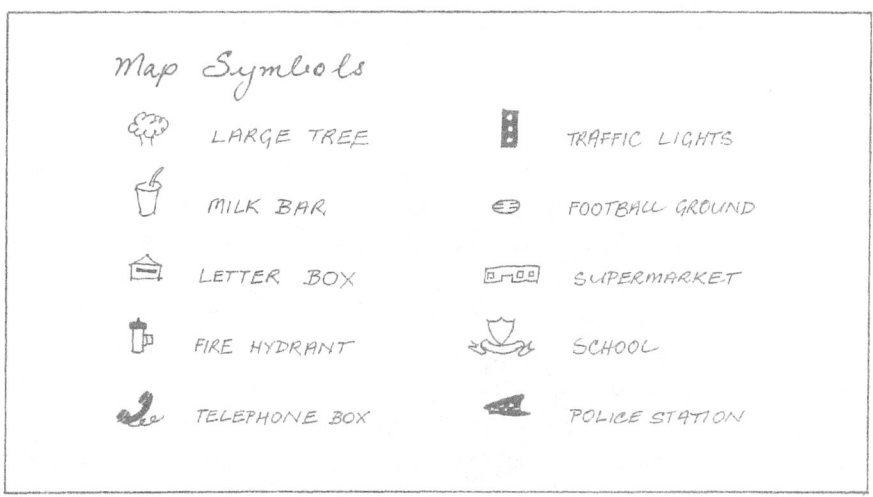

LEVEL 5   **LESSON 15**

NAVIGATION:
COMPASS USE (INTRODUCTION)

Aim

To introduce the compass and its main features.

Equipment

- One orienteering compass per student

Activity

Encourage the students to find out as much as they can about the compass for approximately five minutes.

Ask them what they have discovered about it. These features can be listed and then drawn on the chart.

Points to look for are:
- The round dial
- The numbers, 0–360
- The red needle always points the same way
- The four letters on the dial, N, S, E, W
- The direction arrow.

The students should all find each of the features listed. Establish where the red needle points and that no matter which way you turn the compass, it will still point north.

The students, in pairs, take turns in finding different numbers that are multiples of ten. At this stage it is not important to use numbers that are not multiples of ten.

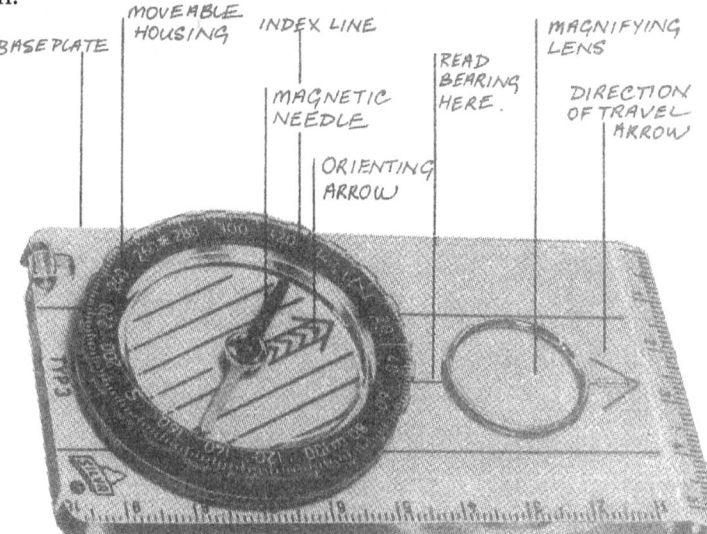

62

LEVEL 5   LESSON 16

NAVIGATION: COMPASS USE

Aim

To understand the concepts of compass use.

Equipment

- Enough compasses for each student

Activities

Through experiment, the students should be able to discover that the red needle does not work effectively when held vertically or at an angle, i.e. the compasses are to be held horizontally. The students should also see what happens to the red needle when held near a match or something metallic.

The correct method for holding the compass is demonstrated by the teacher. The students should then see the need to use it carefully to ensure accurate reading.

Have the students practise reading the fine markings on the dial, i.e. each mark represents 2° and odd 10s are not numbered but are marked. All the features of the compass should be recognised.

The next step is for the students to be able to set the compass on one of the four principal directions (N, S, E, W) and, holding the compass at chest height, in the palm of the hand and with the direction arrow pointing away, move to face the direction. This can be done in pairs with each student taking turns to set their partner the task.

NAVIGATION: COMPASS USE

Aim
To enhance compass use.

Equipment
- Enough compasses for each student

Activities
Have the students practice the use of the compass so that they can set a compass to read or to take a bearing, i.e. this means that they are able to turn themselves to have the orienteering arrow aligned with the red (north) needle.

From the previous lesson (of setting the compass to the four compass points), introduce other bearings.

Have each student set their partner a compass-setting task and then make sure that the other gets the compass set correctly.

Ensure that the compass is set carefully and accurately and that it is held flat. Also, the compass should be held next to the chest. To face the correct bearing the whole body is turned – not just the compass.

LEVEL 5   LESSON 18

NAVIGATION: REVISION

Aim
To further practice compass reading and setting.

Equipment
- Enough compasses for each student

Activity
This lesson is for revision and enrichment of the previous lesson.

It is important to revise all aspects of compass setting and direction finding. Give the students plenty of practice.

NAVIGATION: COMPASS WALK

Aim
To enhance the use of the compass.

Equipment
- Enough compasses for each student

Activity
Practise more difficult bearings, particularly those that do not show numbers on the dial. After a reasonable amount of proficiency is gained, set the students a few simple bearing walking tasks, e.g.
180° – walk 6 steps
90° – walk 8 steps
270° – walk 10 steps

This can be done in the classroom and the students can see where they finish. They may have different starting points and observe their finishing points.

This activity can then be extended outdoors and the students, with their partners, can make up their own tasks.

LEVEL 5 LESSON 20

NAVIGATION: COMPASS POINTS

Aim

To develop skills in orienteering through simple compass games.

Equipment
- Compasses – one per student
- Compass game cards 1A (one per student) – Appendix page 144
- Compass game area marked as per Appendix page 141

Activity

After setting up the area each student is given a card. The instructions are very clear and easy to follow.

In these exercises, give the students a starting point and, if they read their compasses carefully, they should finish at the appropriate finishing point.

The students complete the three problems on their cards. When all answers are correct, cards are swapped, and each student works through another card.

GAME **1A**

STARTING POINT 5
NORTH FOR 10 m : EAST FOR 20 m
SOUTH FOR 10 m.

STARTING POINT 6
NORTH FOR 23 m : WEST FOR 8 m
SOUTH FOR 23 m.

STARTING POINT 7
NORTH FOR 13 m : EAST FOR 8 m
SOUTH FOR 13 m.

LEVEL 5　　　　　　　　　　　　　　　　　　　　　LESSON 21

ROPES:
KNOTS

Aim

To revise and expand the student's knowledge of knots.

Equipment
- Various lengths of ropes
- Various thicknesses of ropes and cords

Activity

Four basic knots, each with their own specific applications, are revised from Levels 3 and 4: Lesson 19. These knots are:
- A clove hitch for securing a rope firmly to a pole or stick to prevent the pole from slipping
- A reef knot for securing rope ends together
- A figure of 8 knot which provides a knot that can be used along the length of the rope
- A half hitch for securing any end to ensure a knot will not loosen (see page 40 for diagrams of these knots.)

Stress to the students that all these knots are extremely effective, and that they can be easily undone.

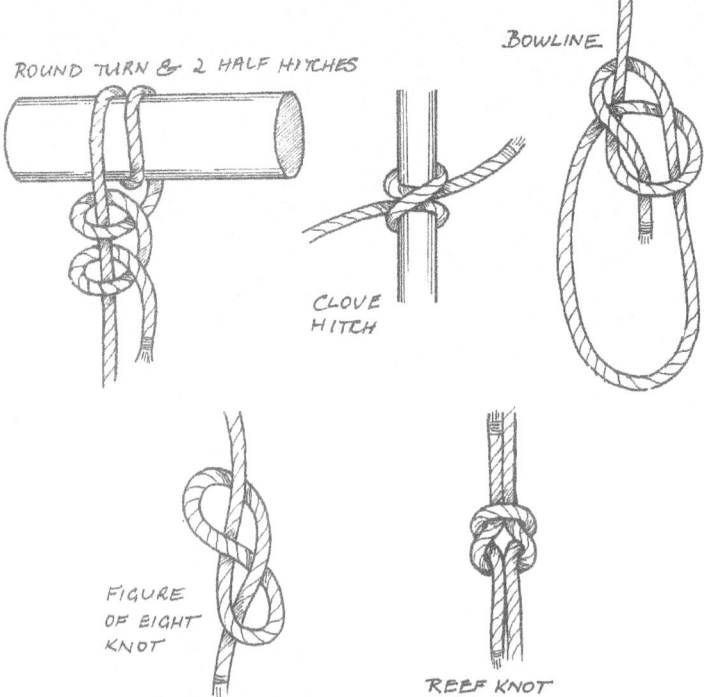

LEVEL 5 LESSON 22

ROPES:
ROPE BRIDGES

Aim
To use previously learned skills with ropes in practical situations.

Equipment
- 3 or 4 sets of ropes, each set containing ropes of varied lengths and thicknesses

Activity
This is simply a task-solving problem whereby each group (of which there may be three or four) are given a set of ropes. Each group must then select an appropriate site to build a rope bridge using the knots they have been taught.

It may be possible to set rules, e.g.
- The bridge must be at least 2 metres in length;
- It must be at least 0.5 metre off the ground;
- There must be at least 4 ropes involved; and
- At least 1 of each of the knots learned must be used.

Possible sites may include between equipment on the adventure playground, between poles in a covered way, between trees, etc.

The Final Test – the bridge must support each member of the group as they cross it.

NB These bridges must not be more than 1 metre above the ground and they must be tested by the teacher before any student is allowed on.

LEVEL 5   **LESSON 23**

BUSHCRAFT: FIRE LIGHTING

Aim

To instil a basic knowledge of fire lighting and to emphasise the safety precautions involved.

Equipment

- Enough kindling for 3 fires
- Newspaper
- Larger wood
- Matches
- 3 buckets of water

Activity

Three basic types of fires can be set:

- Tee-pee
- Box
- Layer.

The box and layer fires can be constructed in a trench.

Each type has its own advantages, e.g. tee-pee will light quickly if the wood is dry. The box type is good for wood that may be damp where the top pieces have time to dry before needed by the fire. The trench fire is an excellent cooking fire. If constructed properly, it allows cooking utensils to be supported by the dirt sides of the trench.

The tee-pee is constructed with paper and kindling in a 'tee-pee' formation. As the kindling burns down, the heavier wood is added.

The box is constructed with paper. The wood is built up in parallel pairs, first two one way, the next two at 90 degrees. Again, heavier wood is added.

The trench fire is set in a trench, of one shovel width and up to 1 metre in length. The fire should take up the entire trench.

The underlying feature of this lesson is safety. Only one person should light the fire and emphasis should be given to the fact that fire is not a toy.

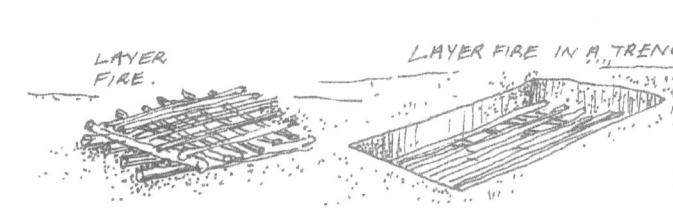

LEVEL 5   **LESSON 24**

BUSHCRAFT: CAMPFIRE

Aim

To provide enrichment in the use of campfires.

Equipment
- Firewood for 3 fires
- Shovel
- Matches
- Newspaper

Activity

After demonstrating the different types of fires (from the previous lesson), each of the three groups is given one type of fire. The group must effectively construct and light its fire.

Prior to each fire being lit, it is important that the construction is checked to ensure that it has been done correctly. One student should then be given the matches in each group and then the fires can be lit.

Safety again is of paramount importance and the teacher should stress that misbehaviour will not be tolerated.

Naturally, the proof of a properly constructed fire will lie in whether it lights or not.

As an extra bonus, potatoes in foil or apples may be placed in the fire and eaten later.

LEVEL 5   LESSON 25

BUSHCRAFT: PROBLEM-SOLVING IN FIRE LIGHTING

Aim

To provide a task with definite limitations to enrich the skills previously learned.

Equipment

Matches

Activity

Again each group must build its own fire. However, this time no paper is supplied and each group is given two matches and a match box.

The purpose behind this is to encourage the lighting of a fire with available materials and with maximum efficiency.

If wood is not available, make a small supply available. But, encourage the conservation of supplies of matches and kindling.

Stress that grass, leaves and bark can replace paper.

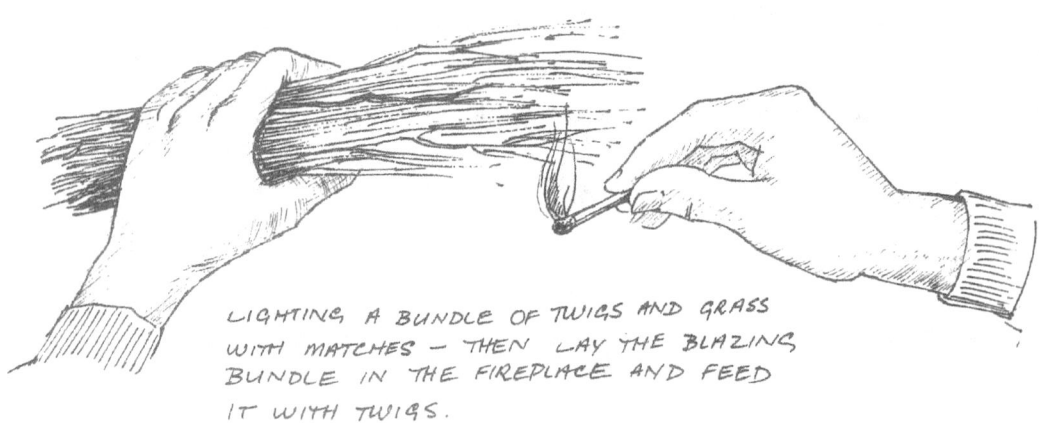

LIGHTING A BUNDLE OF TWIGS AND GRASS WITH MATCHES — THEN LAY THE BLAZING BUNDLE IN THE FIREPLACE AND FEED IT WITH TWIGS.

LEVEL 6

No.	Legend	Theme	Subject
1.	♣	Environmental Studies	Soil
2.	♣	Environmental Studies	Rocks
3.	♣	Environmental Studies	Sensory Trail
4.	♣	Environmental Studies	Gardens
5.	♣	Environmental Studies	Man-made Signs
6.	🗺	Mapping	Symbols
7.	🗺	Mapping	Symbols
8.	🗺	Mapping	Draw Map of Locality
9.	🗺	Mapping	Scale
10.	🗺	Mapping	Scale
11–13.	🗺	Mapping	Scale Map of the School
14–15.	🗺	Mapping	Scale Map of Local Features
16.	🗺	Mapping	Compass Walk on Graph Paper
17.	✸	Navigation	Map from Dictation
18.	✸	Navigation	Compass Use
19.	✸	Navigation	Walk a Bearing
20.	✸	Navigation	Walk a Bearing
21.	✸	Navigation	Walk a Bearing
22.	✸	Navigation	Bearing from a Map
23.	✸	Navigation	Point-to-Point Bearings
24.	✸	Navigation	Route Choice in Travel
25.	✸	Navigation	Distance Ready Reckoner
26–30.	✸	Navigation	Compass Games

LEVEL 6   LESSON I

ENVIRONMENTAL STUDIES: SOIL

Aim

To collect and examine various soils and to discuss rock decomposition.

Equipment
- Variety of soils
- Variety of rocks (local)
- Glass jars

Warm Up (optional)

Arm and thumb wrestle in classroom.

Activity – Part One

Discuss the variations in soils and ground surface, and the way in which soils are made from rock decomposition and erosion.

Activity – Part Two

Groups or pairs of students gather soil samples from the schoolground. Examine the samples and have them described by the group.

Activity – Part Three

Have the groups come together for a class discussion of the samples located. Keep the samples.

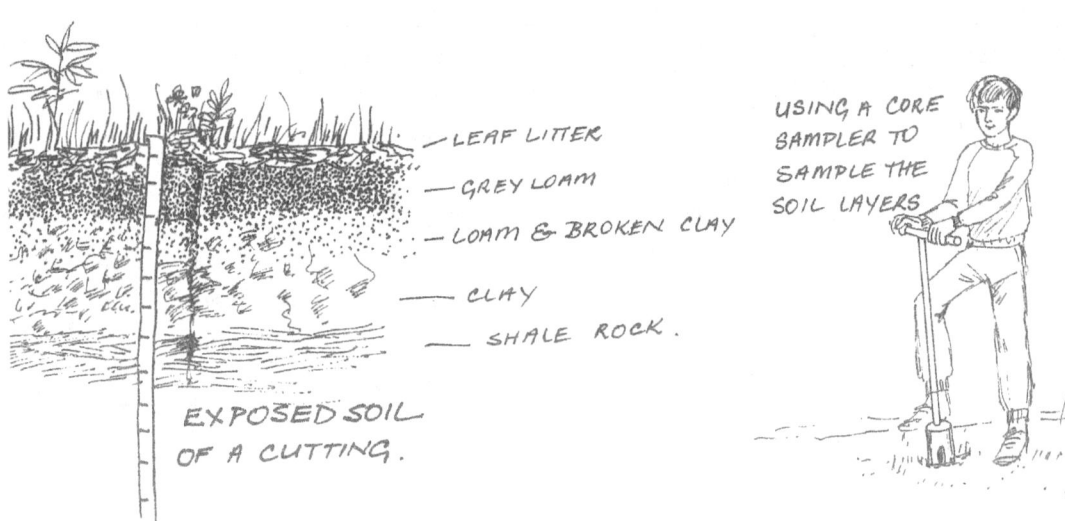

LEVEL 6   *LESSON 2*

ENVIRONMENTAL STUDIES: ROCKS

Aim

To introduce different types of rock and to use soil samples from Lesson 1 for related activities.

Equipment
- Soil and rock samples (Lesson 1)
- Glass jars

Warm Up (optional)

Students complete ten each of sit-ups, push-ups and 'burpees'.

Activity – Part One

Review the soil samples from Lesson 1. Introduce and discuss different types of rock, e.g. igneous, sedimentary, metamorphic.

Activity – Part Two

Using small quantities of soil samples, have the students construct a 'layered' sedimentary 'rock' within their glass jars.

Activity – Part Three

The students present their 'layered rock' to the class.

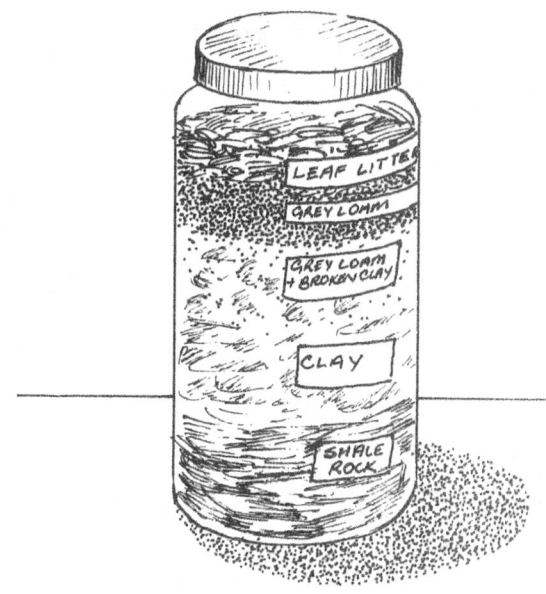

LEVEL 6   *LESSON 3*

ENVIRONMENTAL STUDIES: SENSORY TRAIL

Aim

To practise recognising our environment without the use of sight.

Equipment

- Blindfolds (1 between 2 students)
- Ball of string

Warm Up

Any 'chasey' game.

Activity – Part One

Discuss our senses and how we rely so much on our sight. Explain the sensory trail activity.

Activity – Part Two

The sensory trail activity is marked out by string. The students pair off, one student is blindfolded. The 'blind' student follows the string around the playground. Their partner asks the blindfolded student to feel and smell objects, trees, etc. in an attempt to identify them. The students then change places.

The 'sighted' student may direct their partner along any path (trail) they want.

Activity – Part Three

Return to the classroom to discuss any difficulties. Ask the students, 'How much harder would it be in an unfamiliar environment, e.g. the bush?'

LEVEL 6　　　　　　　　　　　　　　　　　　　LESSON 4

ENVIRONMENTAL STUDIES: GARDENS

Aim

To study nearby gardens and to evaluate their worth from the point of view of a native bird or animal.

Equipment

- Some photos of gardens
- Diagrams of the five individual garden areas seen as advantageous to birds and animals

Warm Up

A short run.

Activity – Part One

Discuss the planned lesson with the students. Many suburban gardens are ideal for attracting native birds and animals. Some of these visitors will stay for long periods if there is sufficient shelter, food and breeding-places. One way to measure the qualities of a garden is by awarding 'stars'. A 'Five Star' garden will have:

1. An earth, rock or wood litter space for ground feeders and scratchers;
2. Three or more large flowering native shrubs as shelter and food for small ground animals;
3. A large area of grass, herbs or low shrubs for nectar feeders and insectivores;
4. A visible watering place for bird bathing and drinking;
5. At least one tall tree above the roof line for roosting and nesting of larger birds.

Activity – Part Two

In pairs, the students assess the gardens of houses in a nearby street(s), giving them a 1, 2, 3, 4 or 5 star rating.

Activity – Part Three

Have the students compare their ratings with other pairs who have assessed the same garden.

LEVEL 6　　　　　　　　　　　　　　　LESSON 5

ENVIRONMENTAL STUDIES: MAN-MADE SIGNS

Aim

To introduce students to, and make them aware of, the great number of signs in our environment.

Equipment
- Prepare a route through the nearby streets which have interesting sign posts
- A map (with a list of appropriate questions)

Warm Up (optional)

Aerobic exercise.

Activity – Part One

Discuss with the students the number and types of signs that they see in their day-to-day life. Draw a large map of the planned walk to show students the intended route and to explain the activity.

Activity – Part Two

In pairs, students follow the route, answering the questions. Examples of the types of questions to be asked are:
- Find the number of the MMBW water meter.
- Find the small metal plate and number on the SEC pole.
- What word is on the letter box at No. 8 Erin Street?
- When is it against the law to park in Main Road?

NB Part Two can be completed without leaving the classroom. The students can remember the signs that they pass on their way to school.

Activity – Part Three

Students compare their findings.

LEVEL 6　　　　　　　　　　　　　　　　　　　　　LESSON 6

MAPPING: SYMBOLS

Aim
To revise the mapping symbols covered in Level 5.

Equipment
- Duplicated sheets of map symbols

Warm Up (optional)
Follow the Leader aerobics.

Activity – Part One
Explain and discuss the identification of map symbols, their purposes and universal usage.

Activity – Part Two
Have the students match the symbol with its name, or draw the symbol next to its name.

Symbols

- HARD SURFACE HEAVY DUTY HIGHWAY
- HARD SURFACE HIGHWAY, MEDIUM TRAFFIC
- IMPROVED DIRT ROAD
- UNIMPROVED DIRT ROAD
- TRACK
- ROAD BRIDGE
- FOOT BRIDGE
- FORD
- SINGLE RAILWAY TRACK
- DOUBLE RAILWAY TRACK
- BUILDINGS
- HOUSES
- SCHOOL
- CHURCH
- CEMETERY
- TELEPHONE LINE
- POWER LINE
- QUARRY OR MINE
- LAKE
- STREAM
- SPRING
- WELL
- SWAMP
- BUSH
- ORCHARD
- SCRUB
- CLIFF
- FENCE
- DEPRESSION
- GRAVEL PIT

LEVEL 6   LESSON 7

MAPPING: SYMBOLS

Aim
To reinforce the use of map symbols.

Equipment
- A class set of a photo or picture of a country scene
- A set of grids on which the maps are to be drawn

Warm Up (optional)
Any 'chasey' game.

Activity – Part One
Show the students copies of the picture and briefly identify, as a group, the major points of interest.

Activity – Part Two
Have the students complete their grid map of the picture using map symbols.

Activity – Part Three
View the maps and discuss any problems.

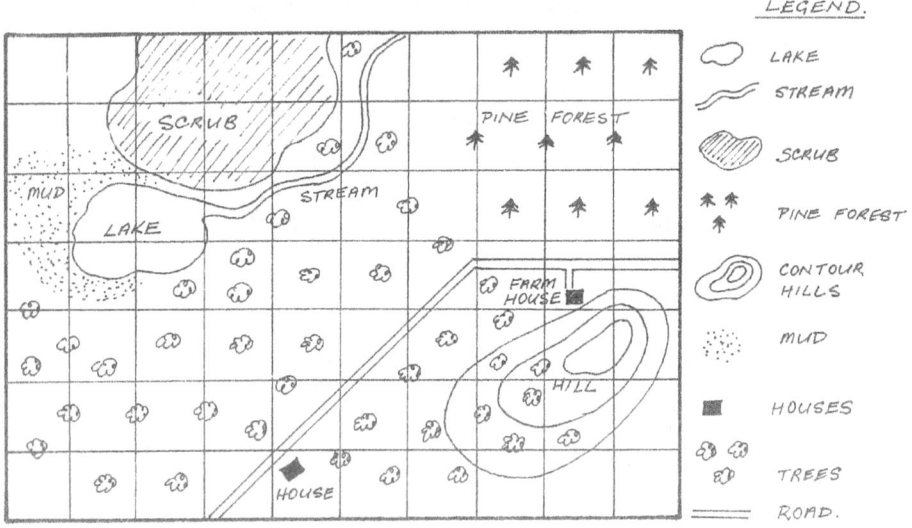

LEVEL 6 *LESSON 8*

MAPPING:
DRAW MAP OF LOCALITY

Aim

To use map symbols while constructing a map of the local area.

Equipment
- Paper
- Pens
- Pencils

Warm Up (optional)

Run around the school.

Activity – Part One

Briefly review the map symbols talked about in the previous lesson. Draw an outline (with the student's help) of the local environment to be included in the student's maps.

Activity – Part Two

Each student completes a map of the local area using the map symbols. The map should include the school and nearby streets, houses, shops, etc.

Activity – Part Three

Complete the teacher's map on board with the student's help.

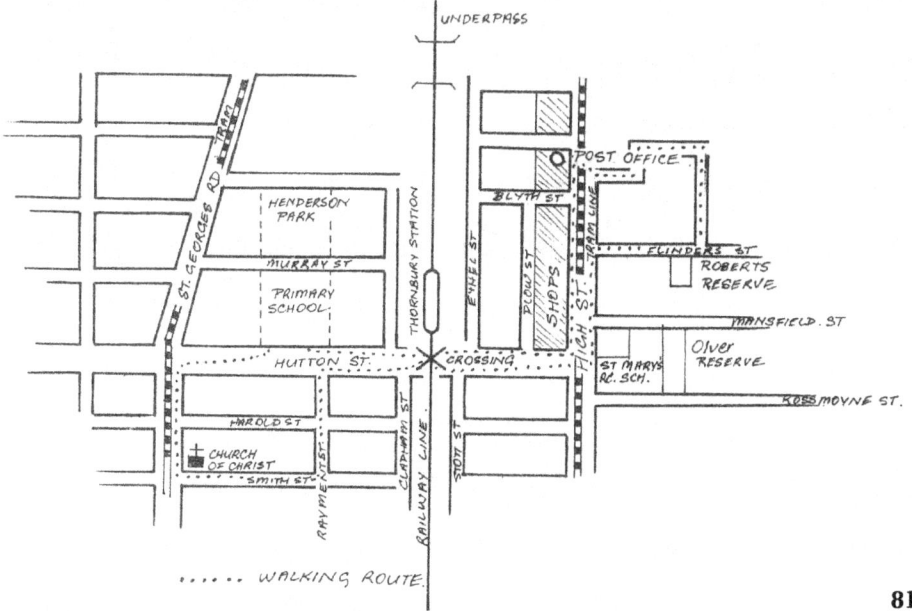

LEVEL 6 — LESSON 9

MAPPING: SCALE

Aim
To introduce the concept of scale.

Equipment
- Maps from previous lessons
- Examples of different types of published maps
- A class set of one map (from a street directory)

Warm Up (optional)
Flexibility exercises.

Activity – Part One
Refer to the student's own maps from the previous lesson, and point out the need for a scale for all maps. A scale ensures correct proportion of all areas shown and enables the person to calculate the exact sizes of buildings and distances of roads, rivers, etc. Show the students examples of the published maps.

Using examples, explain the mathematics involved in calculating the scale of a map. Show the different ways in which scale may be written: 1 : 100,000 or $\frac{1}{100,000}$

Activity – Part Two
Using the class set of one particular scaled map, set students problems to solve using the scale, e.g.
- 1 cm on the map is equivalent to … in real terms?
- How far is the school from the railway line?
- How long is Camp Road?

Activity – Part Three
Review the idea of scale. Check the student's answers.

LEVEL 6   LESSON 10

MAPPING: SCALE

Aim
To revise the idea of scale by drawing a scale map of the classroom.

Equipment
- Rulers
- Measuring tapes
- Large sheets of paper or cardboard

Warm Up (optional)
Any running game.

Activity – Part One
Briefly review the concept of scale and test the student's understanding. Explain the activity and group the students into small groups.

Activity – Part Two
Within their groups, the students measure the room and the pieces of furniture. Each group determines a scale for its map and draws a full-scale map of the classroom.

Activity – Part Three
The groups present their maps to the class. Discuss whether each group used the same scale.

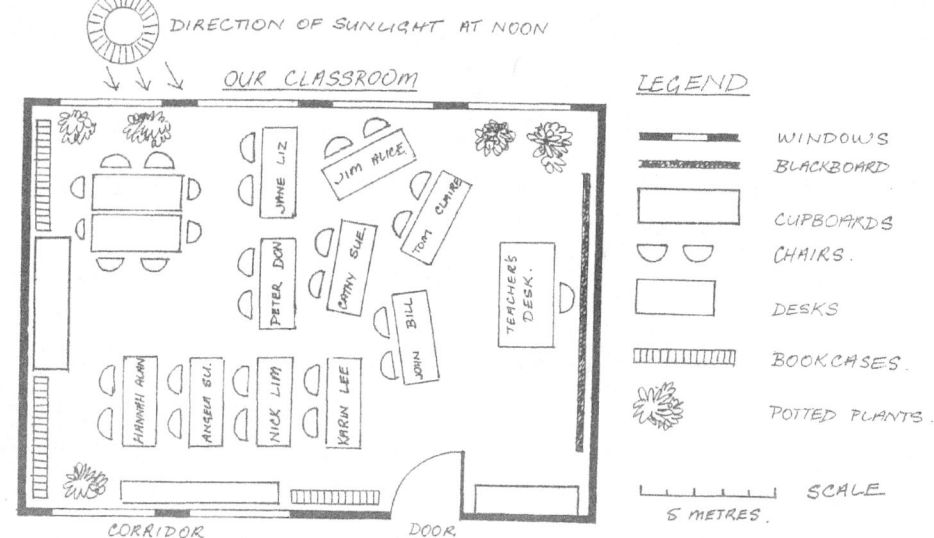

LEVEL 6 — LESSONS 11, 12 AND 13

MAPPING: SCALE MAP OF THE SCHOOL

Aim

To further develop the understanding of scale by producing models of the schoolground.

Equipment
- Trundle wheels
- Measuring tapes
- Construction materials

Warm Up

Activities on suspension equipment.

Activity – Part One

Explain the activities to be completed. Place student in groups of five or six. The groups will need to be large enough to ensure the completion of the task in three lessons (approximately 1½ hours).

Activity – Part Two
Lessons 12 and 13

The teacher sets the scale for the project. In their groups, the students measure the perimeter of the schoolground. They also measure the buildings, calculating distances from buildings to fences and playground areas, etc. They then produce a scale model using cardboard boxes, papier mache, paints, textiles, etc.

Activity – Part Three

Groups present their completed models to the class.

LEVEL 6　　　　　　　　　　　　　　　　　　LESSONS 14 AND 15

MAPPING: SCALE MAP OF LOCAL FEATURES

Aim

To complete a map of the local environment (as for Lesson 8) using a scale and the map symbols identified from Lessons 6, 7 and 8.

Equipment
- Maps from Lesson 8
- Cardboard
- Trundle wheels

Warm Up

Exercises to music.

Activity – Part One
Lesson 14

Refer back to the student's maps to establish the area to be included. Discuss ways of measuring the area by the students pacing it out (e.g. 1 large step = 1 metre) or by using trundle wheels.

Appoint certain sections of the area to particular students and have them measured, e.g. John and Maria might determine the size of the park, Gail and Bruno might measure the length of three streets.

Activity – Part Two
Lesson 15

In pairs or small groups, the students set off to measure the local environment. This will require strict supervision by the teachers involved.

When the students have recorded the distances, a master copy is placed on the chalkboard for all to refer to.

Each student then completes their own scaled map of the area using the universal map symbols.

If leaving the schoolgrounds is unpractical, the same exercise can be done by estimation.

LEVEL 6 LESSON 16

MAPPING:
COMPASS WALK ON GRAPH PAPER

Aim
To revise the eight major directions of the compass.

Equipment
- Graph paper

Warm Up (optional)
Tail Tiggy

Activity – Part One
Revise the major points of the compass on a compass star – N, S, E, W, NE, NW, SE and SW.

Activity – Part Two
On their graph paper, the students trace out a 'compass walk'. The directions may be given orally, may be written on the chalkboard or presented on a duplicated sheet, e.g. Begin at a common point then 2N, 3E, 1NW, 2NE, 1N, 2W, 5N, 9E, 6S, 2SW, 1 SE, 4W, etc.

The exercise could be attempted using a scale, e.g. 20mN, 30E, 10NW, 20NE, 10N, 20W, 50N, 90E, 60S, etc.

Activity – Part Three
Discover if anyone became 'lost' while on the 'walk'.

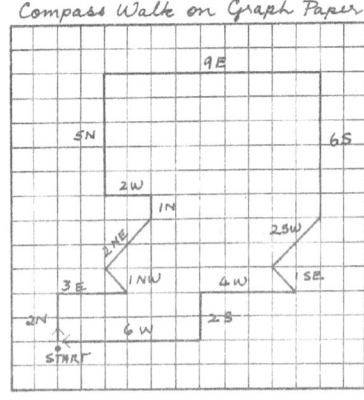
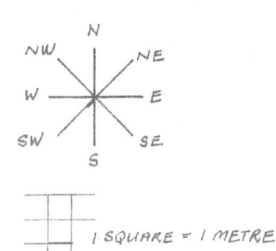

LEVEL 6 — LESSON 17

MAPPING: MAP FROM DICTATION

Aim

To reinforce the concepts of scale, compass directions and map symbols, and to evaluate student's understanding of these.

Equipment
- Paper
- Class sets of description (optional)

Activity – Part One

Explain the activity and briefly revise the symbols. Have each student draw the boundary of their map and establish the scale.

Activity – Part Two

Have the students draw a map from a description which is given orally or in written form. The map must be to scale and must make use of all appropriate map symbols.

Activity – Part Three

The teacher may collect the maps for evaluation purposes.

Sample map and example of descriptions.
Scale 1 cm = 200 metres
e.g. Power lines run across the map from W. to E. 200 m S of the northern border. A major road runs parallel to the power lines 200 m south of them. A minor road runs due south off the major road, 1600 m from the eastern boundary. A school is situated in the SE corner of this road junction, etc.

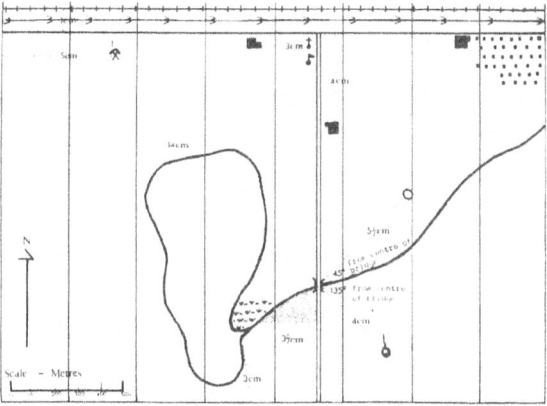

LEVEL 6 — LESSON 18

NAVIGATION: COMPASS USE

Aim

To revise the parts of an orienteering compass and become familiar with each part's purpose.

Equipment
- Orienteering compasses

Warm Up (optional)

Some vigorous outside activity.

Activity – Part One

Ideally, each student should be given their own compass to study. Explain the parts of the compass and their purposes:
- Scales
- Base plate
- Compass housing with dial and orienteering lines
- Magnetic needle
- North of dial
- Direction-of-travel arrow
- Magnifying lens
- Index pointer (black line for bearing point)
- Orienteering arrow (in housing)
- Dial graduation

Activity – Part Two

Conduct some simple activities in the classroom, e.g.:
- Discover where North is.
- What direction (approximately) does your table face?

At this point, the teacher should revise with the students the correct way of holding the compass, i.e. horizontally, close to the chest.

LEVEL 6 *LESSON 19*

NAVIGATION: WALK A BEARING

Aim
To practise moving along a bearing.

Equipment
- Orienteering compasses

Warm Up
Here, There, Where using direction names – N, S, E, W.

Activity – Part One
Revise the parts of the compass and give instructions on how to set a bearing:
- Hold the compass flat in the palm of one hand until the required numerical marker is directly over the index pointer.
- Holding the compass at your chest, with the direction-of-travel arrow pointing directly ahead, turn your body around slowly, until the orienteering arrow is aligned with the magnetic needle.
- Look directly ahead along the path of the direction-of-travel arrow to discover a landmark in the distance.
- Head for that landmark.

Activity – Part Two
Have the students move along the bearings as set by teachers outside in the playground.

NAVIGATION: WALK A BEARING

Aim

To teach, and have the students practise, taking sight bearings.

Equipment
- Orienteering compasses

Warm Up

Arm, thumb and leg wrestles.

Activity – Part One

Review setting and walking along a bearing. Instruct the students on how to take a sight bearing:
- Align the direction-of-travel arrow so it points directly at the chosen landmark.
- Carefully turn the compass housing until the magnetic needle (north end) is directly above the orienteering arrow. The degree measurement directly over the index pointer is the bearing for that landmark from that particular point.

Stress that if each student takes their bearing from a different position, the answers will differ.

Activity – Part Two

The students answer problems as posed by the teacher, e.g.:
- What is at 200° from the goal post?
- What is at 181° from the front steps?

LEVEL 6 LESSON 21

NAVIGATION: WALK A BEARING

Aim

To have students practise walking, setting and taking bearings.

Equipment

- Orienteering compasses

Warm Up

Aerobic dance routine.

Activity – Part One

Revise taking bearings as shown in the previous lesson. Pair the students and then have two pairs working together.

Activity – Part Two

Have the students set problems as activities for their accompanying pair. For instance, Pair A may first discover the bearing for a landmark in the distance and then ask Pair B to work out what that landmark is.

Activities may involve walking along the bearings.

This lesson is similar to Lesson 20 except that the students, rather than the teacher, pose the problem.

LEVEL 6　　　　　　　　　　　　　　　　　　　LESSON 22

NAVIGATION: BEARING FROM A MAP

Aim
To teach students how to take a bearing from a map, i.e. a point-to-point bearing.

Equipment
- Compasses
- Sample north-lined paper

Warm Up (optional)
An obstacle run.

Activity – Part One
Explain how, by using a map and knowing where you are, the bearing of any destination can be determined. Place the side edge of the compass along the line from present position to destination, ensuring that the direction-of-travel arrow is pointing in the correct direction. The housing is then turned until the orienteering arrow points to North on the map; it will be parallel to the vertical grid lines on the map. This is the bearing.

Activity – Part Two
Using sample north-lined paper, the students determine bearings for imaginary destinations.

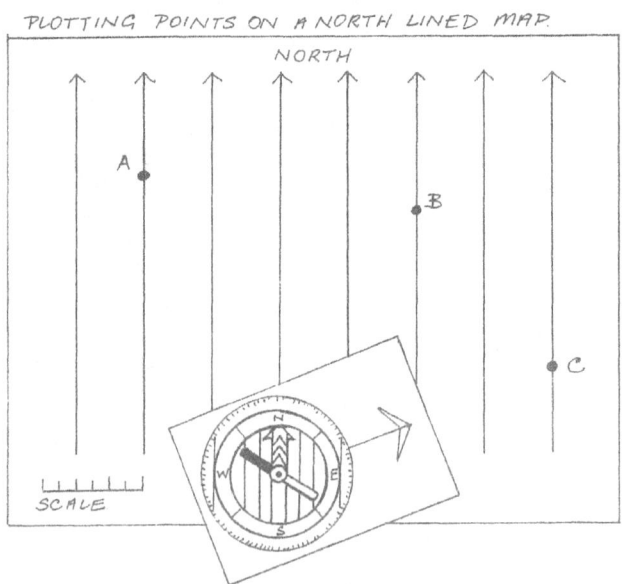

LEVEL 6   *LESSON 23*

NAVIGATION: POINT-TO-POINT BEARINGS

Aim
To practise taking point-to-point bearings.

Equipment
- Compasses
- Copies of maps from Lesson 17

Warm Up (optional)
Any 'chasey' game.

Activity – Part One
Examine the maps and revise the map symbols. Revise how to take a point-to-point bearing using an example from the map.

Activity – Part Two
Students determine the bearings of landmarks on a map, e.g.: the shelter shed from the canteen.

Activity – Part Three
Correct any problems while going over the process.

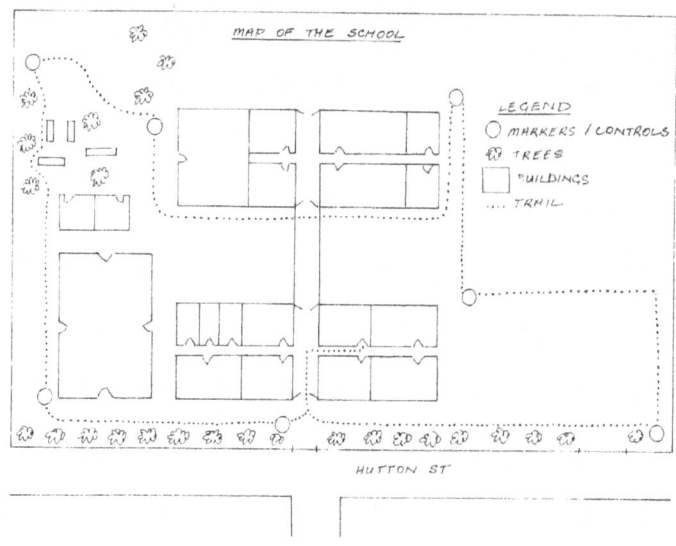

LEVEL 6 — LESSON 24

NAVIGATION: ROUTE CHOICE IN TRAVEL

Aim

To determine how to get around obstacles that lie directly along a desired path.

Equipment
- Sample maps with obstacles drawn in
- Compasses

Warm Up (optional)

Activities on playground equipment.

Activity – Part One

Either distribute samples of maps or draw one on the chalkboard with an obstacle (open paddock) lying on the point-to-point route. Discuss with the students how they would get around this: from the original point, locate a landmark on the far side of the obstacle, and continue to head for that landmark.

If the obstacle obstructs the line of sight, then select a new point, perhaps the corner of the building, take a new point-to-point bearing from the map, and then walk to a new landmark.

Activity – Part Two

Pose problems for the students to answer.

LEVEL 6   LESSON 25

NAVIGATION: DISTANCE READY RECKONER

Aim
To determine the average walking and running step of each student.

Equipment
- A marked-out distance of 100 metres
- Ready reckoners

Warm Up
Exercises to music.

Activity – Part One
Revise with the students the idea of scale and how the actual distance from a map is determined. Explain that if we have to travel 65 metres, we must know the length of each one of our steps.

Activity – Part Two
Students walk the 100 m distance two or three times and then, by referring to the ready reckoner, discover the average length of their steps for future reference. Repeat the activity with running steps.

Activity – Part Three
Ready reckoners are then made for the number of steps a child takes per metre, e.g. the average for 100 m is eighty running steps. See pages 142–143 for more information about distance ready reckoners.

READY RECKONER FOR RUNNING	
Metres	**Steps**
100	80
50	40
25	20
10	5
5	4
Approx. 3	2
1	1

LEVEL 6   **LESSON 26-30**

NAVIGATION: COMPASS GAMES

Aim

To practise using compasses by completing compass games 1A, 1B, 2A, 2B and 3A.

Equipment
- Compasses
- Copies of compass games
- Marked out area for games

Warm Up

Any suitable vigorous activity.

Lesson 26

Games 1A Cards 1-6

Lesson 27

Games 1B Cards 1-6

Lesson 28

Game 2A Cards 1-6

Lesson 29

Game 2B Cards 1-6

Lesson 30

Game 3A Cards 1-6

Teaching Points
1. For ease of reference, one metre is equivalent to one big walking step.
2. A student stays on one card until all three problems have been successfully completed, and then proceeds to another card at the same level.

LEVEL 7

No.	Legend	Theme	Subject
1.	✹	Navigation	Revision
2.	✹	Navigation	Compass Games
3.	✹	Navigation	Compass Games
4.	✹	Navigation	Bearing and Clue Course
5.	✹	Navigation	Bearing and Clue Course
6.	✹	Navigation	Bearing and Distance Course
7.	✹	Navigation	Bearing and Distance Course
8.	✹	Navigation	Sketch Map Course
9.	✹	Navigation	Sketch Map Course
10.	✹	Navigation	Grid Reference
11.	✹	Navigation	Map Grid Course
12.	✹	Navigation	Map Grid Course
13.	🔍	Initiative Activities	Blindfold Order
14.	🔍	Initiative Activities	Electric Fence
15.	🔍	Initiative Activities	Limited Legs
16.	👍	Signalling	Semaphore Code
17.	👍	Signalling	Semaphore Code
18.	👍	Signalling	Semaphore Code
19.	👍	Signalling	Morse Code
20.	👍	Signalling	Morse Code
21.	⛺	Bushcraft	Tent Pitching (small tents)
22.	⛺	Bushcraft	Tent Pitching (large tents)
23.	⛺	Bushcraft	Bush Telephone
24.	⛺	Bushcraft	Water Collection
25.	✺	Ropes	Basic Knots

26.	✿	Ropes	Basic Knots
27.	✿	Ropes	Knots and Bridges
28.	✿	Ropes	Rope Bridges
29.	✿	Ropes	Rope Bridges
30.	✿	Ropes	Rope Bridges
31.	✿	Ropes	Basic Lashings
32.	✿	Ropes	Lashing Constructions
33.	✿	Ropes	Lashing Constructions
34.	✿	Ropes	Lashing Constructions
35.	✿	Ropes	Lashing Constructions

LEVEL 7   **LESSON 1**

NAVIGATION: REVISION

Aim

To revise the basic techniques of compass use.

Equipment

- Orienteering compass per student
- Ground marking of compass games as outlined in the Appendix p. 141

Warm Up

1. Astride jumps/arms raising sideways.
2. Astride jumps/arms raising forwards.
3. Patterns of astride jumps.

Activity – Part One

Revise:

- The basic use of a compass.
- How to set a bearing.
- How to walk a bearing.

Activity – Part Two

Instead of using a ready reckoner to establish stride length, as in the lessons in previous levels, now estimation is the key. It should be practised until one long walking step is equal to one metre. This whole navigation section of Level 7 should then be completed on this 1:1 ratio.

Students complete a Game 1A and a Game 1B card of compass games (three problems on each card).

Example

Game 1A

1. Starting point 1
   Directions: North for 10 m, East for 15 m, South for 10m.
2. Starting Point 1
   North for 2 m, East for 25 m, South for 2 m.
3. Starting point 1
   North for 18 m, East for 10 m, South for 18 m.

LEVEL 7 LESSON 2

NAVIGATION: COMPASS GAMES

Aim

To revise fine skills of compass use in the form of the compass games as outlined in the Appendix p. 141.

Equipment
- 1 orienteering compass per student
- Ground workings of compass games
- 1 compass game card per student

Warm Up (optional)
1. Astride jumps/alternate arm raising one to the side and one to the front.
2. Patterns of these activities.

Activity – Parts One and Two

Students work their way through one card of each of the compass games 2A, 2B and 3A. Each game card increases in difficulty. The student should successfully complete the three problems on each card.

Examples of Game Cards

	Game 2A		Game 2B		Game 3A
1	Starting point 6 0° for 18 m 270° for 7 m 225° for 25.5 m	1	Starting point 5 360° for 10 m 270° for 10 m South-West for 14 m	1	Starting point 3 310° for 10 m 73° for 29 m 225° for 21 m
2	Starting point 6 45° for 7 m 270° for 25 m 225° for 7 m	2	Starting point 5 360° for 18 m 270° for 2 m South-West for 25.5 m	2	Starting point 3 342° for 19 m 120° for 24 m 180° for 6 m
3	Starting point 6 315° for 14 m 90° for 15 m 180° for 10 m	3	Starting point 5 45° for 14 m North-West for 7 m 225° for 21 m	3	Starting point 3 80° for 20 m 278° for 30 m 180° for 7 m

LEVELS 7   LESSON 3

NAVIGATION: COMPASS GAMES

Aim

To revise the skill of taking a bearing from a map and the application of this skill.

Equipment
- 1 orienteering compass per student
- 1 compass game card per student
- Ground workings of compass games

Activity – Part One

1. Revise the practice of taking a bearing from a map using a mini map. The compass is placed on the map (game card) with one edge of the base plate aligned from point-to-point. The 'direction of travel' arrow points to the intended destination. The compass housing is turned until the north lines of the map and those on the bottom of the housing are equal. The bearing is read where it states: 'Read bearing here'.
2. Revise the practice of measuring distance by using scale.

LEVELS 7 — LESSON 4

NAVIGATION: BEARING AND CLUE COURSE

Aim
To extend compass skills into a basic navigation course within the confines of the schoolgrounds.

Equipment
- Previously designed 'bearing and clue' course
- 1 compass per student
- Control card per student (i.e. a copy of the course)

Warm Up
Jog round the school.

Activity – Parts One and Two
1. Issue copies of the course to the students.
2. Explain the procedure.
3. Allocate start times.

Teaching points
1. Students work in pairs.
2. Start the course one minute apart.
3. One partner of each pair should have a watch.
4. Give a final 'come in' time.

Sample Bearing and Clue Course

1. 73° Fence corner
2. 240° Tree
3. 122° Mound of dirt
4. 225° Fence corner
5. 262° Corner building
6. 210° Fence corner
7. 310° Fence corner
8. 32° Corner of building
9. 296° Fence
10. 120° Door

A. Name _____

B. Start time _____

C. Finish time _____

D. Total time _____

LEVEL 7 LESSON 5

NAVIGATION: BEARING AND CLUE COURSE

Aim
To continue the augmentation of compass skill development with a clue and bearing course.

Equipment
- A course set by two students in the class
- 1 compass and 1 control card per student

Activity – Parts One and Two
Students complete the bearing and clue course as in Lesson 4.

Tips in Course Setting
1. Start outside the door generally used by the students.
2. Choose control features that can be seen from each preceding control.
3. Two people set the bearings and then 'split the difference' to get a final bearing.
4. Place controls high enough to be out of reach of students.
5. Avoid possible outside working areas.

SETTING THE BEARING ON A CONTROL

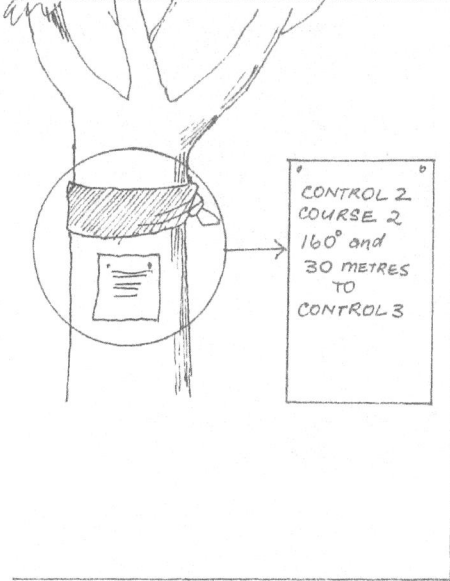

CONTROL 2
COURSE 2
160° and
30 METRES
TO
CONTROL 3

LEVEL 7   LESSON 6

NAVIGATION: BEARING AND DISTANCE COURSE

Aim
To extend navigation skills, emphasising 'step counting', while walking a bearing.

Equipment
- Previously designed 'bearing and distance' course (within the schoolground)
- Compass and 1 control card per student

Warm Up
Jog around the school.

Activity – Parts One and Two
1. Issue control cards and compasses.
2. Explain the procedures.
3. Allocate the start times.

Teaching Points
1. This is a slower course so often it is better taken over a period of one school time block, e.g. 9.05 a.m. – 10.25 a.m. The students can then start every ten minutes.
2. When the distance is covered the navigator should 'circle' in order to find the control.

Sample Bearing and Clue Course:

1. 230° for 104 metres _____   A. Name _____
2. 180° for 107 metres _____
3. 80° for 70 metres _____   B. Start time _____
4. 193° for 62 metres _____
5. 176° for 100 metres _____   C. Finish time _____
6. East for 250 metres _____
7. 270° for 31 metres _____   D. Total time _____
8. 352° for 172 metres _____
9. 320° for 57 metres _____

LEVEL 7   *LESSON 7*

NAVIGATION:
BEARING AND DISTANCE COURSE

Aim

To have students complete a bearing and distance course made by their peers.

Equipment
- A course set by two students who are competent at maths
- 1 compass and 1 control card per student

Activity – Parts One and Two

Students complete the bearing and distance course as in Lesson 6.

Tips in Course Setting
1. Bearings should be taken considering the same points mentioned in Lesson 5 for a bearing and clue course.
2. Use a trundle wheel to measure distance.
3. Do not place controls on metal objects.
4. Make the controls 'easy to see'.
5. Use a pencil and tape to put both letters and control letters on the markers.

LEVEL 7   LESSON 8

NAVIGATION: SKETCH MAP COURSE

Aim

To extend both mapping and navigation skills by using a sketch map of the school.

Equipment

- Teacher-drawn sketch map of the school
- Markers which have been put out
- Master map (showing the location of controls)
- 1 map per student

Warm Up

Simple exercises at tables.

Activity – Part One (inside)

1. Identify features on the map.
2. Teach students how to orientate the map (i.e. hold the map concurrent to the features).
3. Students practise transcribing features from a master map.

Activity – Part Two (outside)

Have the students complete the sketch map course.

Procedure

a. Start.
b. Copy controls from master map.
c. Complete the course recording control letters next to the appropriate circle on the student's own map.

LEVEL 7　　　　　　　　　　　　　　　　　　　　LESSON 9

NAVIGATION:
SKETCH MAP COURSE

Aim
To have students complete a sketch map course made by their peers.

Equipment
- A course set by two students from the class
- 1 map per student

Activity – Parts One and Two
Students complete the sketch map course as in Lesson 8.

Teaching Points
1. Use the two students that set the course to check that the master maps are transcribed correctly.
2. Controls must be taken in sequential order.
3. Ten controls are adequate for all these navigation courses.

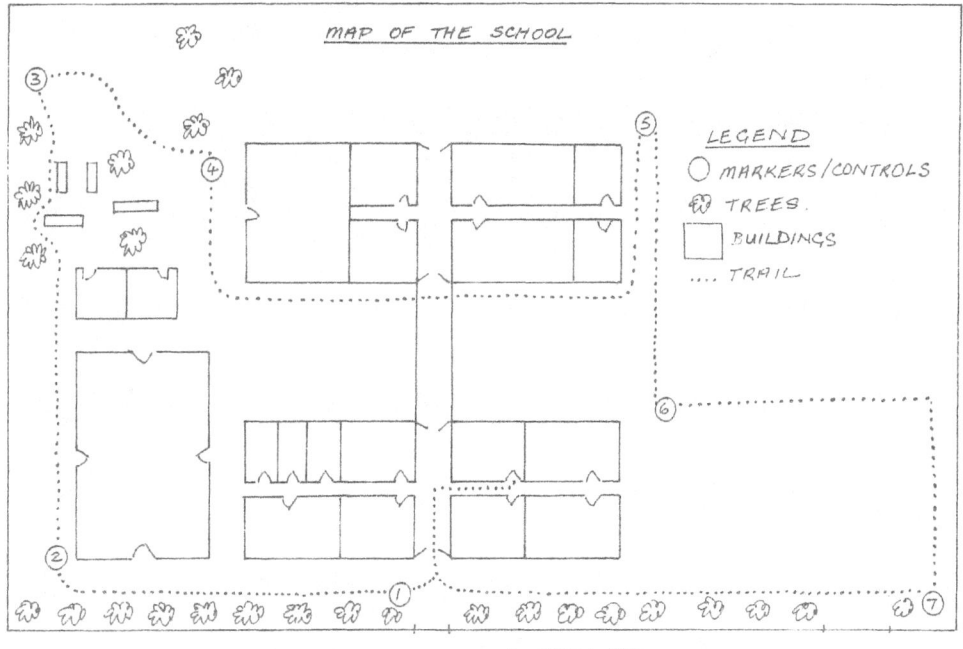

LEVEL 7   LESSON 10

NAVIGATION: GRID REFERENCE

Aim

To teach the grid reference system.

Equipment

- Adequate number of street directories (ideally 1 per student)
- Adequate number of atlases (ideally 1 per student)

Activity – Part One (inside)

1. Using street directories explain the vertical and horizontal system of grid referencing.
2. Go through the features on a common map.
3. Students complete an exercise designed to improve simple grid references.

   Sample: Name the features at:

   Page 21 – L6

   Page 62 – B9

   Page 12 – D3

Activity – Part Two (inside)

Follow a similar procedure with atlases as was completed with the street directories.

LEVEL 7

LESSON 11

NAVIGATION: MAP GRID COURSES

Aim
To complete a navigation course using the grid reference system.

Equipment
- A grid superimposed over the sketch map
- 1 map per student
- Markers placed in obvious positions

Activity – Parts One and Two
Students complete the grid map course. (Procedures are similar to those outlined in the other navigation courses.) The one exception is that when given the reference numbers, e.g. L3, the students shade in the appropriate square.

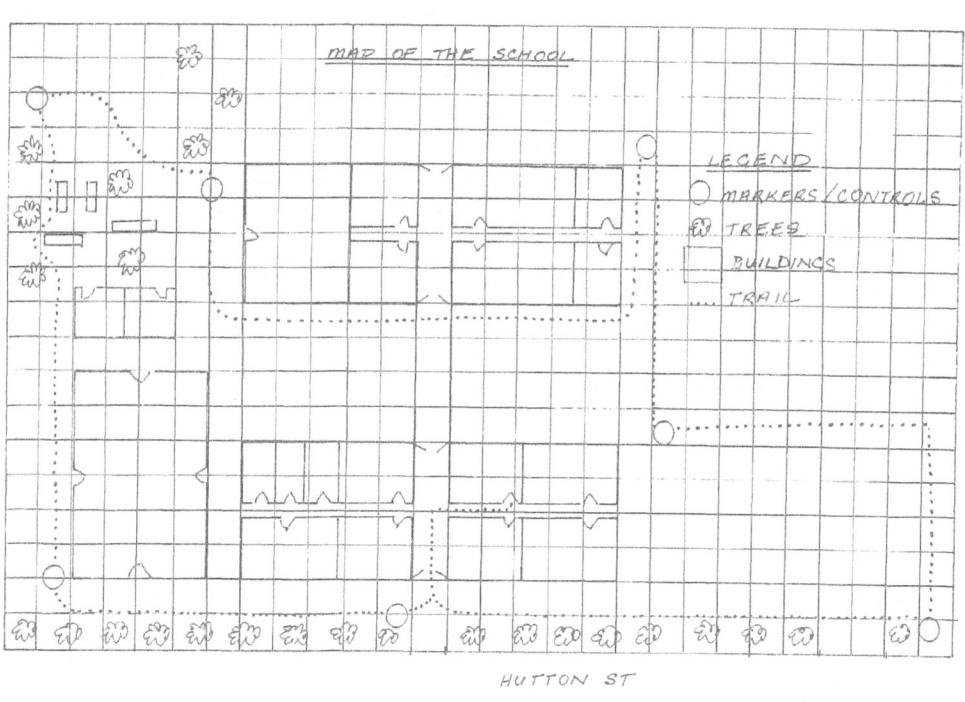

NAVIGATION: MAP GRID COURSE

Aim
To complete a grid map course as made by students within the class.

Equipment
- 1 grid map per student
- Course designed and set up.

Activity – Parts One and Two
Students complete the grid map course as in Lesson 11.

Teaching Points
- Orientate the map.
- Shade in all reference squares before starting.
- Record marker letters within the appropriate grid square.
- Markers for this course should vary in height above the ground.

LEVEL 7 **LESSON 13**

INITIATIVE ACTIVITIES: BLINDFOLD ORDER

Aim
To develop personal initiative and group cooperation.

Equipment
- Blindfolds for all members of the class

Warm Up (optional)
Clumps
For this game the students have to make up groups containing the number as called out by the teacher. Those left over lose one point.

Activity – Part One
Blindfold Line
a. All students are blindfolded and sitting in random order. The teacher moves among the class giving each student a number. (This is done by a tap on the shoulder and verbally telling each student.)
b. The object of this exercise is then for the class to move into a single line without using sight or verbal communication.
c. When the students believe they are in a ranked line, they link arms and sit down. The students then disclose their correct numbers.

Activity – Part Two
Blindfold Circle
The same procedure as for Blindfold Line can be used to form a circle.

Blindfold Figure of Eight
This is played similarly to the previous two games.

LEVEL 7   LESSON 14

INITIATIVE ACTIVITIES: ELECTRIC FENCE

Aim
To develop lateral thinking and group cooperation.

Equipment
- String tied (1 metre high) between climbing frames or trees to form a pen
- Strong pole
- 2 m long and 9 cm in diameter

Warm Up
Jog around obstacle course or fitness track.

Activity – Part One
All the students are in the 'electrified' pen. The object of the game is to get the entire class over the electric fence. The pole starts inside the pen.

Activity – Part Two
The game can be varied by having group competitions and/or by raising the height of the string.

LEVEL 7 **LESSON 15**

INITIATIVE ACTIVITIES: LIMITED LEGS

Aim
To develop personal initiative and group cooperation.

Equipment
- 2 lines 10 m apart

Warm Up
Jog around obstacle course or the fitness track.

Activity – Part One
Six Legs
The class is divided into groups of five to seven. The aim is for the group to cover the 10 m distance in a specified manner. In this case, the restrictions are:
- There are only six points of contact with the ground for the entire group;
- That the group must be in contact with each other throughout the entire crossing.

Activity – Part Two
Five Legs, Four Legs
The game can be varied by adding further restrictions or by changing combinations of the groups.

LEVEL 7   LESSON 16

SIGNALLING:
SEMAPHORE CODE

Aim
To introduce the skills of signalling with flags and to improve hand/eye coordination and laterality.

Equipment
- Flags – one pair for each two students (made by students)
- Cards containing the semaphore code (1 for each student)

Activity – Part One (inside)
The basic semaphore code is explained and the method of notation (interpretation) is practised.

Activity – Part Two (outside)
In pairs, approximately 100 m apart, one student signals a letter and the partner has to record. Check to see if correct. Students then swap actions. The procedure is repeated for simple words.

A	B	C	D	E	F
G	H	I	J	K	L
M	N	O	P	Q	R
S	T	U	V	W	X
Y	Z	ERASE	SIGNALLING USING THE SEMAPHORE CODE.		

A	B	C	D
E	F	G	H
I	J	K	L
M	N	O	P
Q	R	S	T
U	V	W	X
Y	Z	ERASE	

LEVEL 7 LESSON 17

SIGNALLING: SEMAPHORE CODE

Aim
To continue signalling using flags.

Equipment
- 1 pair of flags between 2 students
- A semaphore card (as in Lesson 16 – flag positions for each letter) for each student

Activity – Part One (inside)
The teacher signals a word and the students record. This signalling can be gradually increased in pace to improve the student's memory of the chart.

Activity – Part Two (outside)
Students are in pairs 100 m apart. They signal letters (that do not make words) in groups of six. Similar signalling can be tried using arms only, instead of flags.

SIGNALLING THE LETTER "R"

LEVEL 7 *LESSON 18*

SIGNALLING: SEMAPHORE CODE

Aim

To continue signalling using flags.

Equipment

- Flags
- 10 pairs
- Semaphore cards

Activity – Parts One and Two (inside/outside)

The students are divided into three equal teams. Teams 1 and 2 remain in the classroom, team 3 is stationed around the school buildings, so that a message can be sent around the school.

Team 2 selects a five-letter word and gives this to the leader of Team 3. The leader then starts the signalling process of this word.

The final member of Team 3 does not have any flags, but simply records the final signals.

Team 1 then selects a word for Team 2, and Team 3 selects a word for Team 1.

LEVEL 7 LESSON 19

SIGNALLING: MORSE CODE

Aim

To introduce the skills of signalling using Morse code.

Equipment

- Mirrors or rulers – 1 between two students
- A card of Morse code for each student

Activity – Part One (inside)

Explain the basic Morse code and practise the method of notation (interpretation).

Activity – Part Two (rulers inside mirrors outside):

In pairs, approximately 100 m apart, one student signals a letter and the partner has to record. This is done for five letters, then the records are checked and the students swap activities. A dash is a long flash; a dot is a short flash.

Using a ruler, dots are taps on the edge, dashes are taps by the flat of the ruler.

A	· —	W	· — —
B	— · · ·	X	— · · —
C	— · — ·	Y	— · — —
D	— · ·	Z	— — · ·
E	·		
F	· · — ·	1	· — — — —
G	— — ·	2	· · — — —
H	· · · ·	3	· · · — —
I	· ·	4	· · · · —
J	· — — —	5	· · · · ·
K	— · —	6	— · · · ·
L	· — · ·	7	— — · · ·
M	— —	8	— — — · ·
N	— ·	9	— — — — ·
O	— — —	0	— — — — —
P	· — — ·		
Q	— — · —		
R	· — ·		
S	· · ·		
T	—		
U	· · —	*Morse Code*	
V	· · · —		

LEVEL 7   LESSON 20

SIGNALLING: MORSE CODE

Aim
To continue signalling using Morse code.

Equipment
- Mirrors or rulers – 1 for each student
- 1 Morse code card for each student

Activity – Parts One and Two
Words and numbers are signalled in pairs. Again the distance apart should be approximately 100 m. Using rulers, dots are taps on the edge, dashes are taps by the flat of the ruler.

TAPPING OUT MORSE CODE WITH A RULER
TAP WITH THE EDGE FOR A DOT, WITH THE FLAT FOR A DASH.

LEVEL 7   *LESSON 21*

BUSHCRAFT:
TENT PITCHING (SMALL TENTS)

Aim

To introduce the skills of tent pitching and to improve fine motor coordination and group cooperation.

Equipment
- Tents - preferably two-person tents
- Appropriate number of mallets, ropes and pegs

Activity – Part One (inside)

Explain the procedure of pitching a tent.
1. Clear ground.
2. Close openings in tent.
3. Peg corners of tent floor.
4. Peg around bottom of tent, to form a tight rectangle.
5. Raise the end poles or ridge poles and secure with guy ropes.
6. Peg and tighten all side ropes.
7. Adjust guys to get even tautness.

Activity – Part Two (outside)

Divide the class into groups according to the number of tents. The tents are then pitched according to the recommended procedure.

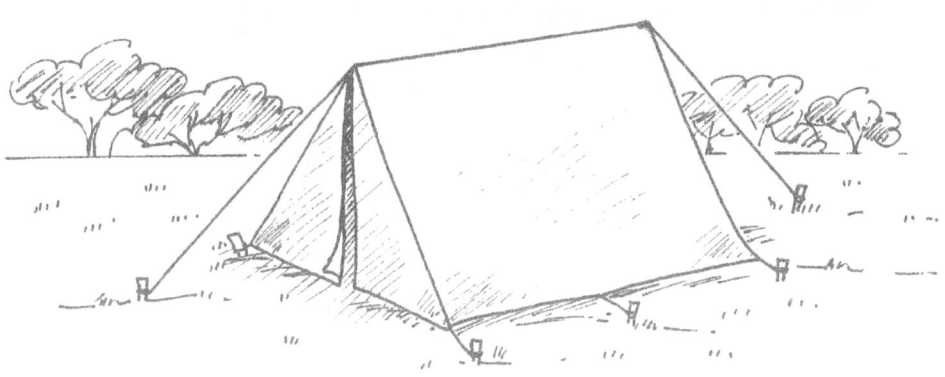

LEVEL 7 LESSON 22

BUSHCRAFT:
TENT PITCHING (LARGE TENTS)

Aim

To continue to introduce the skills of tent pitching using large tents.

Equipment
- Large tents – ideally 4 six-person tents
- Accompanying gear

Activity – Parts One and Two

Divide the class into groups according to the number of tents. The tents are then pitched according to the recommended procedure.

Variation

Tent pitching can be varied by using different styles of tents, e.g.
- Outside frame
- Inside frame
- 'A' frame
- Side poles

Extension

Pitching tents while all but one student in the group is blindfolded. The sighted student is not permitted to work, but merely give instructions.

LEVEL 7   LESSON 23

BUSHCRAFT:
BUSH TELEPHONE

Aim
To construct and use a bush telephone

Equipment
- Several hammers and nails
- 2 tin cans and 50 m of string between each two students

Activity – Part One (inside)
Explain the procedure for making a bush telephone:
1. Punch a small hole in the end of each tin.
2. Thread the string through both holes.
3. Tie a large knot in the string, inside the tin. This prevents the string being pulled out.

Activity – Part Two (outside)
Students use bush telephone from 50 m apart. The string should be tight and not touch anything or anyone.

Variations can be tried in different locations.

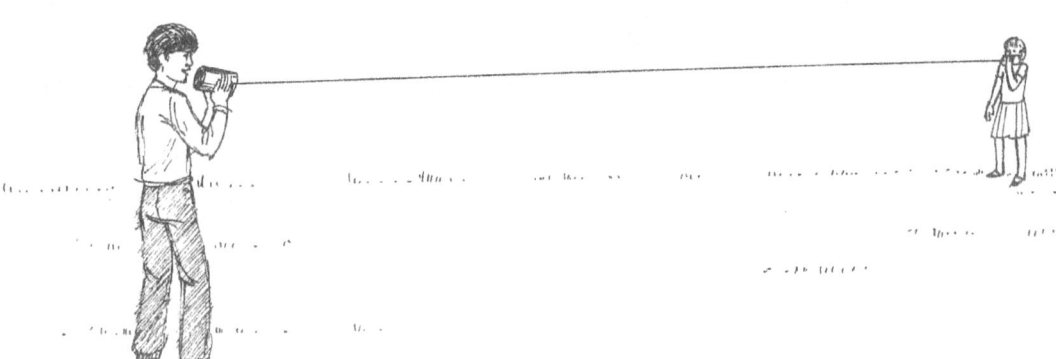

LEVEL 7   *LESSON 24*

BUSHCRAFT: WATER COLLECTION

Aim

To collect moisture in a solar still.

Equipment

- 2 sheets of 1 m X 2 m plastic
- 2 water containers
- 2 'hand size' stones
- 2 holes or 2 digging implements

Activity – Part One (inside)

Explain the procedure for making a solar still.
1. Dig a hole with sides sloping at 45°.
2. Place a water container at the bottom of the hole.
3. Place leaves and plants around the container.
4. Place the plastic sheet over the hole and secure the edges with soil.
5. Place a rock in the middle of the plastic so that it lies directly above the tin.

Activity – Part Two (outside)

Divide the students into groups and have them construct solar stills.

Activity – Part Three (outside)

Preferably, the solar stills should be made at the start of the school day, so that the results can be inspected at the end of the school day.

LEVEL 7   **LESSON 25**

ROPES:
BASIC KNOTS

Aims
- To revise the tying of the granny and the reef knots, plus a round turn plus half hitches.
- To improve both hand/eye and fine motor coordination.

Equipment
- Ropes 1 or 2 m long – 1 for each student (e.g. skipping ropes)
- Pieces of string 1 or 2 m long for each student

Activity – Part One (inside)
Revise the three knots using explanation, demonstration and diagrams. These knots are practised using the ropes.

Reef Knot
Hold ends of rope.
Left over right and right over left.
Pull tight so ends lie parallel to main rope.

REEF KNOT

Granny Knot
Hold ends of rope.
Left over right and left over right.
Pull tight now ends don't lie parallel to main rope.
This knot slips under pressure, so is a po substitute for a reef knot.

GRANNY KNOT

Round Turn plus Half Hitches
To tie one end to a table leg.
End around upright twice.
Then two half hitches on the main rope.
Half hitch is over and through.

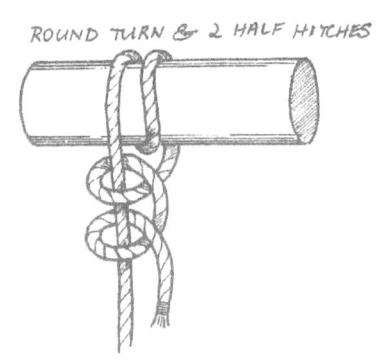

ROUND TURN & 2 HALF HITCHES

Activity – Part Two (inside)
These same knots are practised with the string which requires finer motor coordination.

LEVEL 7   *LESSON 26*

ROPES: BASIC KNOTS

Aim

To teach the basic knots of bowline and slipknot.

Equipment

- One rope and one piece of string per student.

Activity – Part One (inside)

The knots are taught by explanation, demonstration and diagrammatically.

Bowline

The bowline is a good non-slip knot.
Hold the start or the running end of the rope.
Make a loop approximately 60 cm from the end.
The running end goes up through this loop, around the main rope and down through the loop again.
"The rabbit comes out of the burrow, around the tree, and back down the burrow again!"

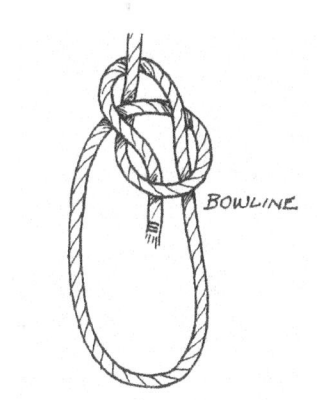
BOWLINE

Slipknot

The slipknot holds firm and is difficult to untie.
The short or running end is taken around the main rope or standing end at least three times.
The short end is passed through the end loop and then back through the second loop just created.
The end is pulled tight and parallel to the main rope.

FISHERMAN'S HOOK KNOT (SLIP KNOT)

Activity – Part Two (inside)

These knots are then practised with string.

LEVEL 7 *LESSON 27*

ROPES:
KNOTS AND BRIDGES

Aim
To introduce the practical application of knot tying to such things as building rope bridges.

Equipment
- Ropes and string for each student for knot tying
- Longer pieces of string, for bridge building, 3 pieces between students

Activity – Part One (inside)
Revise the knots – granny, reef, round turn and two half hitches, bowline, slipknot.

Explain when they are used:
- Granny – by mistake
- Reef – to join ends of one rope
- Turn and hitches – secure a fixed end which will always have tension
- Bowline – a non-slip knot (no tension required to keep tight)
- Slipknot – to secure end that does not need to be untied.

Activity – Part Two (inside)
Tie string between table legs to practise the use of these knots in their correct situation.

LEVEL 7   LESSON 28

ROPES:
ROPE BRIDGES

Aim

To build miniature rope bridges between tables or desks.

Equipment

- String (3 pieces for each 2 students)

Activity – Part One (inside)

Koala Walk

This is a single-strand bridge which can be horizontal or on a slight angle.

Vertical Bridge

This is a two-line bridge. The top rope is directly above the bottom rope and high enough so that it can be comfortably held above a person's head if he or she is standing on the bottom rope.

Tension Traverse

This is a two-line bridge. The bottom rope is tight. The top rope is tied only at one end. To traverse this bridge a person stands on the bottom rope and walks backwards, holding the top rope for balance.

Activity – Part Two (inside)

Burmese Bridge

This is a four-line bridge one to walk on; one either side as hand supports; one laced between the other three ropes to keep them an equal distance apart.

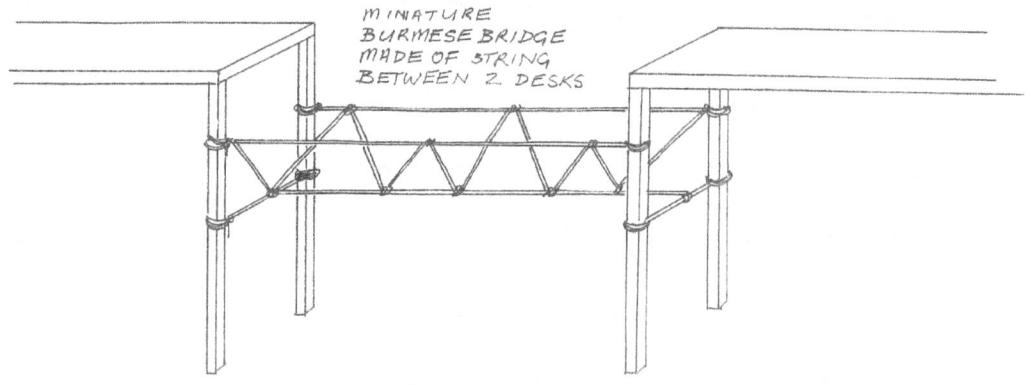

LEVEL 7 **LESSON 29**

ROPES:
ROPE BRIDGES

Aim
To build rope bridges between trees or playground equipment.

Equipment
- Rope – 5 cm in diameter and 12 m long, 2 for each group of 5 students

Warm Up
Join Up Tiggy

Activity – Parts One and Two
The one- and two-line bridges are made between appropriate trees or climbing equipment.
NB: These bridges should be less than 1 m from the ground.

Koala Walk
The students cross the bridge by gripping the single rope with both hands and feet. Hanging underneath the rope while crossing is called the 'Koala Walk'; crawling on top of the rope is called the 'Commando Crawl'. Students use the bridges in both ways.

Vertical Bridge
The students cross this bridge travelling sideways with both feet on the bottom rope and both hands on the top rope.

Tension Traverse
This bridge is crossed travelling backwards, both feet on the bottom rope and both hands holding the loose top rope.

TENSION TRAVERSE
1 METRE

LEVEL 7   LESSON 30

ROPES: ROPE BRIDGES

Aim
To build a four-line rope bridge (Burmese) which requires great group cooperation in tensioning and positioning.

Equipment
- Rope – 5 cm in diameter and 12 m long
- 3 for each group of 5 students
- Twine – 25 m long, 1 per group

Warm Up
Scarecrow Tag

Activity – Parts One and Two
Burmese Bridge
Bottom rope first.
Then two side ropes.
Then laced together using the twine.
Bridge crossed walking forwards, feet on bottom rope and hands on side ropes.

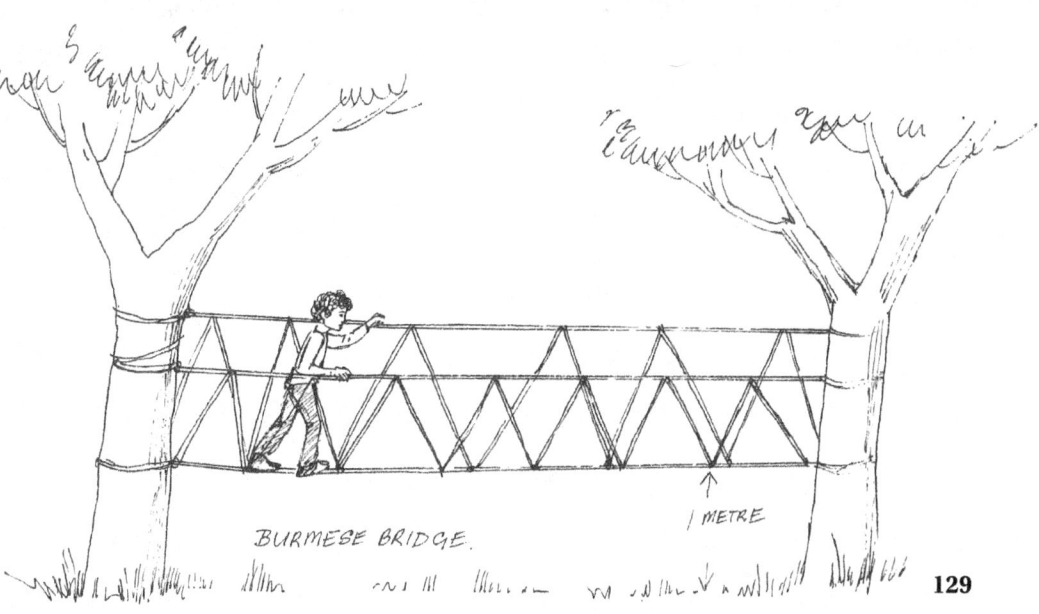
BURMESE BRIDGE.
1 METRE

ROPES: BASIC LASHINGS

Aim
To teach both square and diagonal lashings (this improves fine motor coordination).

Equipment
- String or twine - 1 piece of 5 m for each student
- 2 gymnastic canes for each student

Activity – Part One (inside)
Teach both types of lashings by explanation, demonstration and by diagrams.

Square lashing (right angles)
Tie string to vertical pole.
String goes over the right side of the horizontal, around the vertical (above the horizontal), and down over the left side of the horizontal.
Tension kept on the string at all times.
Each turn is laid flat against its predecessor.
Lashing is finished by three round turns and a reef knot.

Diagonal lashing (not 90°)
Slip knot is tied around both canes at their junction.
End is taken 4 times through the vertical joints and then 4 times through the horizontal joints.
End is turned around each part of each cane to tighten the lashing.
Lashing is finished with a reef knot.

Activity – Part Two
Have students practise both lashings individually and in pairs. The teacher becomes the traditional roving tutor.

DIAGONAL LASHING

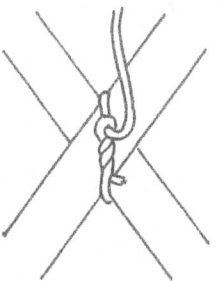
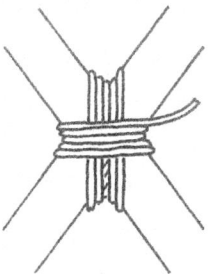

1. TIE A RUNNING BOWLINE OR TIMBER HITCH ROUND BOTH SPARS AT THE ANGLE OF CROSSING.

2. DRAWING THEM TOGETHER, TAKE 3 OR 4 TURNS ACROSS ONE FORK AND 3 OR 4 ACROSS THE OTHER FORK.

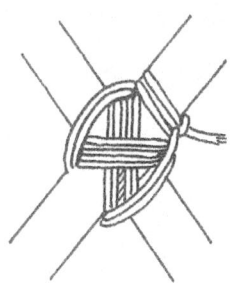

3. AS IN ALL LASHINGS, FRAPPING IS NEEDED TO TIGHTEN IT. FINISH OFF WITH A CLOVE HITCH ROUND THE NEAREST SPAR.

SQUARE LASHING

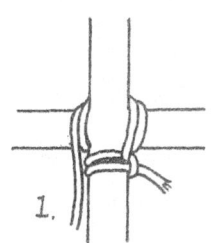
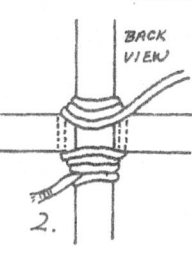
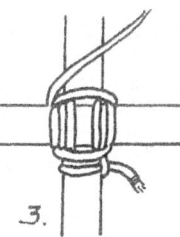
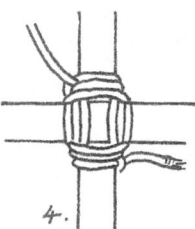

1. BEGIN WITH A CLOVE HITCH, LAY THE HORIZONTAL SPAR ACROSS THE VERTICAL,

2. BRING THE CORD UP AND OVER IT TAKE IT ROUND THE UPRIGHT,

3. ABOVE THE HORIZONTAL AND THEN BRING IT DOWN

4. OVER THE HORIZONTAL UNTIL ONE LASHING IS MADE, REPEAT 4 TIMES. FINISH WITH A REEF KNOT

LEVEL 7 LESSON 32

ROPES: LASHING CONSTRUCTIONS

Aim

To make basic constructions using square lashings.

Equipment

- Many pieces of string
- Boxes of small twigs and sticks

Activity – Parts One and Two (inside)

Make miniature constructions using square lashings. Students can choose from the following

- Ladder
- Pack rack
- Table

Any construction can be made using right-angles only.

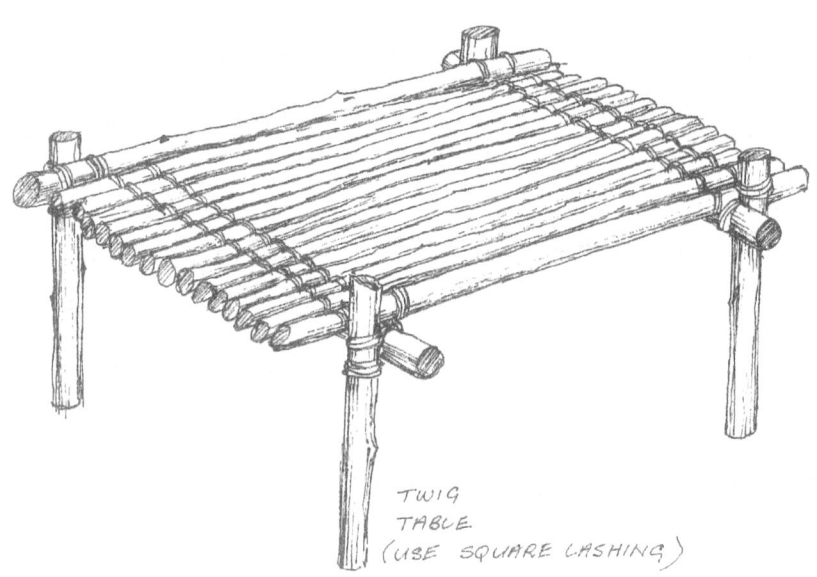

TWIG TABLE
(USE SQUARE LASHING)

LEVEL 7   *LESSON 33*

ROPES: LASHING CONSTRUCTIONS

Aim

To make constructions using diagonal lashings.

Equipment
- Many pieces of string
- Many sticks and twigs

Activity – Parts One and Two (inside)

Make miniature constructions using diagonal lashings. Students can choose from the following:
- Tripod
- 'A' frame.

Using combinations of square and diagonal lashings, make objects such as stretchers, huts, tables, etc.

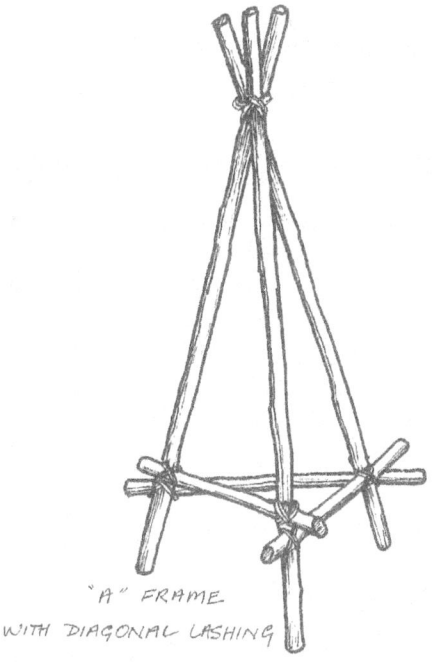

"A" FRAME WITH DIAGONAL LASHING

LEVEL 7   LESSON 34

ROPES:
LASHING CONSTRUCTIONS

Aim
To augment the fine, gross and hand/eye coordination required when making rope constructions on a major scale.

Equipment
- A great deal of string,
- Twine, sticks, poles and canes

Activity – Parts One and Two (outside)
Have students work in pairs to make at least two full-size constructions that have been made in miniature in the previous lessons.

BUSH LADDER

LEVEL 7 *LESSON 35*

ROPES:
LASHING CONSTRUCTIONS

Aim

To make group constructions using lashings.

Equipment

- A great deal of string, twine, sticks, poles and canes

Activity – Parts One and Two (outside)

Group construction bush stretcher (5 students per group).

Tie diagonals to keep main side poles rigid. These are done at both ends of the stretcher using diagonal lashings. Make a bed for the patient by lacing twine between side poles. Lay jumpers on the stretcher bed. Carry the patient on the stretcher.

NB The teacher must check that the stretcher is made strongly enough before any attempt is made to carry a volunteer 'patient'.

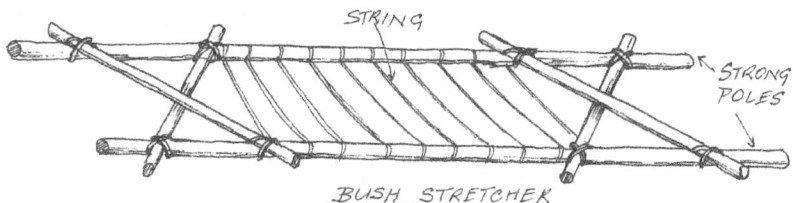

KNOTS

These knots should be taught in the classroom. Diagrams should be displayed as visual reinforcement during the actual tying of the knots. Both video demonstrations and written material are also suitable teaching methods.

The knots should be tied at first in free space (i.e. in the air), then fixed to some object such as the leg of a desk. Partner inspection and assistance between students is essential at this stage.

The following knots are not the complete answer to all problems. They do provide an appropriate knot or group of knots to meet most challenging situations.

Reef Knot

Use
- For tying together the two ends of one piece of rope.

REEF KNOT

Method
- Hold the two ends facing each other with the end in the right hand closer to the body. The right-hand end is taken from the inside over the left-hand end and around it to finish underneath. These two ends are then lifted to face each other again.
- The end now in the left hand is taken inside and over the end now in the right hand end.
- When the knot is finished, the ends should lie parallel. If the ends do not lie parallel it probably means that an insecure 'granny knot' has been tied. This should not be used.

Clove Hitch

Use

- To hitch the middle of the rope to a tree, etc.
- This knot should only be tied in the middle of a rope as continuous strain can 'work free' the running end if this knot is tied at the end of a rope.

Method

- Make a turn around the tree with the running end. Then pass this running end under the standing end and across the standing part. Now the running end is passed again around the tree and back under itself.

A Round Turn and Two Half Hitches

Use

- To attach a rope to a tree, etc. that can be quickly untied.

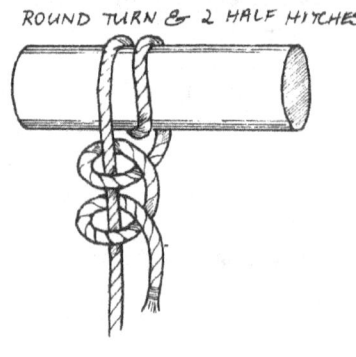

Method

- Take the running end around the tree, this is a single turn. Take this same end around again to complete the round turn. Finally, tie two half hitches around the standing end of the rope to complete the knot.

Bowline

Use

- When a non-slip knot is essential a bowline is used. This is a strong non-slip knot which has minimum detrimental effect on the rope itself.

Method

- Make a loop and hold this loop with the left hand at the junction. With the right hand pass the running end up and through this loop, around the back of the standing end of this rope and back down through this loop again. The running end is then pulled tight. Secure with two half hitches.
- A rhyme that assists in the order of actions is: 'The rabbit comes out of the burrow, around the tree, and back down the burrow again.'

Figure of Eight

Use

- For making a loop at the end of the rope; for attaching a fish hook.

Method

- Double the rope and make loop with the running end.
- The running end is then taken around the back of the standing end and back around to the front. The running end is then passed through the original loop and pulled tight.

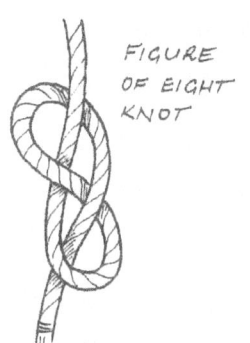

Fisherman's Hook Knot – Slip Knot

Use

- To fix an object securely (e.g. fish hook) and to produce a knot which is impractical to untie.

Method

- The running end makes a large loop and is then wound around the standing end three times. The running end is then passed down through the original loop then back up through the second loop just created. The running end is then pulled tight. The standing end is then pulled in order to slide the knot in contact with the object to be secured.

COMPASS GAMES

As well as being an integral part of a physical education program, many of the activities in outdoor education could be covered in science, geography and art, compass games can be an integral part of a mathematics program.

These compass games have been designed to fit roughly the area of a netball court. They are designed along a west to east control line that is thirty metres long, and with the control points five metres apart.

They can be played:
a. Within the classroom using graph paper.
b. In the school ground using orienteering compasses.

When using graph paper, a small compass rose should be drawn in the top right-hand corner so that the north–south line is vertical. The baseline from left to right equals west to east.

The bottom of the graph must be the control line containing all starting points. The controls must be numbered from west to east (left to right), so that the western end of this control line is starting point one.

Example:
Starting point one
10 metres north, 15 metres east, 10 metres south
Finishing point should be *four*.

When marking out the grid for the games to be played outside, the following procedure is suggested:
1. Set a west to east base line 30 metres long with base controls 5 metres apart.
2. These base controls are assigned numbers 1 to 6.

NB The west-east line must be exact.

Many school netball courts run west–east, so it would be convenient to mark this compass games baseline permanently.

These games can be played on a larger scale by increasing the distance between the baseline controls, course controls and the scale, proportionately.

Ready Reckoner

To play the compass games and the follow up navigation courses the students should know the length of both their average walking and jogging steps. To find these averages, a set distance is marked-out (for example 100 metres); then the students walk (and run) this distance many times. The number of steps taken each lap is recorded. Later in class, the number of steps taken can be averaged, and every student can estimate how many steps they should take for any set distance.

For ease of conversion from metres to corresponding steps, it is suggested that each student have their own conversion chart or 'ready reckoner'. The following 'ready reckoner' calculations can be used to help students make their own 'ready reckoner'. For example, if a student takes 137 walking steps over 100 metres they would refer to the 135 column. It can be then estimated that if they had to walk 20 metres they would need to take 27 steps (both are taken to the nearest number at the head of a column).

Compass Games

To play these schoolground compass games each student should carry: a game card, an orienteering compass and a ready reckoner. On completion of a game 1A card they progress to the next game in the sequence e.g. 1B.

Ready Reckoner

100	100	105	110	115	120	125	130	135	140
1	1	1	1	1	1 ¼	1 ¼	1 ¼	1 ¼	1 ¼
2	2	2	2	2 ¼	2 ½	2 ½	2 ½	2 ¾	2 ¾
3	3	3 ¼	3 ¼	3 ½	3 ½	3 ¾	4	4	4 ¼
4	4	4 ¼	4 ½	4 ½	4 ¾	5	5 ¼	5 ¼	5 ½
5	5	5 ¼	5 ½	5 ¾	6	6 ¼	6 ½	6 ¾	7
6	6	6 ¼	6 ½	7	7 ¼	7 ½	7 ¾	8	8 ¼
7	7	7 ¼	7 ¾	8	8 ½	8 ¾	9	9 ½	9 ¾
8	8	8 ½	8 ¾	9 ¼	9 ½	10	10 ½	10 ¾	11 ¼
9	9	9 ½	10	10 ½	11	11 ¼	11 ¾	12 ¼	12 ½
10	10	10 ½	11	11 ½	12	12 ½	13	13 ½	14
11	11	11 ½	12	12 ½	13 ¼	13 ¾	14 ¼	14 ¾	15 ¼
12	12	12 ½	13	13 ¾	14 ½	15	15 ½	16 ¼	16 ¾
13	13	13 ¾	14 ¼	15	15 ½	16 ¼	17	17 ½	18 ¼
14	14	14 ¾	15 ½	16	16 ¾	17 ½	18 ¼	19	19 ½
15	15	15 ¾	16 ½	17 ¼	18	18 ¾	19 ½	20 ¼	21
16	16	16 ¾	17 ½	18 ½	19 ¼	20	20 ¾	21 ½	22 ½
17	17	17 ¾	18 ¾	19 ½	20 ½	21 ¼	22	23	23 ¾
18	18	19	19 ¾	20 ¾	21 ½	22 ½	23 ½	24 ¼	25 ¼
19	19	20	21	22	23	23 ¾	24 ¾	25 ¾	26 ½
20	20	21	22	23	24	25	26	27	28
21	21	22	23	24	25 ¼	26 ¼	27 ¼	28 ¼	29 ¼
22	22	23	24	25 ¼	26 ½	27 ¼	28 ¼	29 ¾	30 ¾
23	23	24 ¼	25 ¼	26 ½	27 ½	28 ¾	30	31	32 ¼
24	25	25 ¼	26 ½	27 ½	28 ¾	30	31 ¼	32 ½	33 ½
25	25	26 ½	27 ½	28 ¾	30	31 ¼	32 ½	33 ¾	35
26	26	27 ¼	28 ½	30	31 ¼	32 ½	33 ¾	35	36 ½
27	27	28 ¼	29 ¾	31	32 ½	33 ¾	35	36 ½	37 ¾
28	28	29	30 ¾	32 ¼	33 ¼	35	36 ½	37 ¾	39 ¼
29	29	30 ½	32	33 ½	35	36 ¼	37 ¾	39 ¼	40 ½
30	30	31 ½	33	34 ½	36	37 ½	39	40 ½	42
31	31	32 ½	34	35 ½	37 ¼	38 ¾	40 ¼	41 ¾	43 ¼
32	32	33 ½	35	36 ¾	38 ½	40	41 ½	43 ¼	44 ¾
33	33	34 ¾	36 ½	38	39 ½	41 ¼	43	44 ½	46 ¼
34	34	35 ¾	37 ½	39	40 ¾	42 ½	44 ¼	46	47 ½
35	35	36 ¾	38 ½	40 ¼	42	43 ¾	45 ½	47 ¼	49

Compass Games

Game 1A Card 1	Game 1A Card 2	Game 1A Card 3

1 Starting point 1
   North for 10 m
   East for 15 m
   South for 10 m
	1 Starting point 2
	   North for 8 m
	   West for 5 m
	   South for 8 m
		1 Starting point 3
		   North for 18 m
		   East for 20 m
		   South for 18 m

2 Starting point 1
   North for 2 m
   East for 25 m
   South for 2 m
	2 Starting point 2
	   North for 16 m
	   East for 20 m
	   South for 16 m
		2 Starting point 3
		   North for 4 m
		   West for 10 m
		   South for 4 m

3 Starting point 1
   North for 18 m
   East for 10 m
   South for 18 m
	3 Starting point 2
	   North for 12 m
	   East for 10 m
	   South for 12 m
		3 Starting point 3
		   North for 16 m
		   East for 5 m
		   South for 16 m

Game 1A Card 4	Game 1A Card 5	Game 1A Card 6

1 Starting point 4
   North for 10 m
   East for 15 m
   South for 10 m
	1 Starting point 5
	   North for 8 m
	   West for 5 m
	   South for 8 m
		1 Starting point 6
		   North for 18 m
		   East for 20 m
		   South for 18 m

2 Starting point 4
   North for 2 m
   East for 25 m
   South for 2 m
	2 Starting point 5
	   North for 16 m
	   East for 20 m
	   South for 16 m
		2 Starting point 6
		   North for 4 m
		   West for 10 m
		   South for 4 m

3 Starting point 4
   North for 18 m
   East for 10 m
   South for 18 m
	3 Starting point 5
	   North for 12 m
	   East for 10 m
	   South for 12 m
		3 Starting point 6
		   North for 16 m
		   East for 5 m
		   South for 16 m

Answers – Card 1A

Card 1	Card 2	Card 3	Card 4	Card 5	Card 6
1 1–4	1 2–1	1 3–7	1 4–1	1 5–7	1 6–1
2 1–6	2 2–6	2 3–1	2 4–6	2 5–3	2 6–7
3 1–3	3 2–4	3 3–4	3 4–2	3 5–6	3 6–3

Game 1B Card 1	Game 1B Card 2	Game 1B Card 3

1 Starting point 1
   0° for 10 m
   90° for 15 m
   180° for 10 m
	1 Starting point 2
	   0° for 8 m
	   270° for 5 m
	   180° for 8 m
		1 Starting point 3
		   0° for 18 m
		   90° for 20 m
		   180° for 18 m

2 Starting point 1
   0° for 2 m
   90° for 25 m
   180° for 2 m
	2 Starting point 2
	   0° for 16 m
	   90° for 20 m
	   180° for 16 m
		2 Starting point 3
		   0° for 4 m
		   270° for 10 m
		   180° for 4 m

3 Starting point 1
   0° for 18 m
   90° for 10 m
   180° for 18 m
	3 Starting point 2
	   0° for 12 m
	   90° for 10 m
	   180° for 12 m
		3 Starting point 3
		   0° for 16 m
		   180° for 5 m
		   180° for 16 m

Game 1B Card 4	Game 1B Card 5	Game 1B Card 6

1 Starting point 4
   0° for 14 m
   270° for 15 m
   180° for 14 m
	1 Starting point 5
	   0° for 3 m
	   90° for 10 m
	   180° for 3 m
		1 Starting point 6
		   0° for 15 m
		   270° for 25 m
		   180° for 15 m

2 Starting point 4
   0° for 10 m
   90° for 10 m
   180° for 10 m
	2 Starting point 5
	   0° for 18 m
	   270° for 10 m
	   180° for 18 m
		2 Starting point 6
		   0° for 9 m
		   90° for 5 m
		   180° for 9 m

3 Starting point 4
   0° for 11 m
   270° for 10 m
   180° for 11 m
	3 Starting point 5
	   0° for 13 m
	   90° for 5 m
	   180° for 13 m
		3 Starting point 6
		   0° for 15 m
		   270° for 15 m
		   180° for 15 m

Answers – Card 1B

Card 1		Card 2		Card 3		Card 4		Card 5		Card 6	
1	1–4	1	2–1	1	3–7	1	4–1	1	5–7	1	6–1
2	1–6	2	2–6	2	3–1	2	4–6	2	5–3	2	6–7
3	1–3	3	2–4	3	3–4	3	4–2	3	5–6	3	6–3

Game 2A Card 1	Game 2A Card 2	Game 2A Card 3

1 Starting point 1
   0° for 10 m
   90° for 10 m
   135° for 14 m
	1 Starting point 2
	   0° for 2 m
	   45° for 21 m
	   180° for 17m
		1 Starting point 3
		   0° for 6 m
		   90° for 14 m
		   135° for 8.5 m

2 Starting point 1
   0° for 4 m
   45° for 14 m
   180° for 14 m
	2 Starting point 2
	   0° for 15 m
	   90° for 5 m
	   135° for 21 m
		2 Starting point 3
		   0° for 10 m
		   45° for 7 m
		   180° for 15 m

3 Starting point 1
   45° for 21 m
   90° for 14 m
   180° for 16 m
	3 Starting point 2
	   45° for 20 m
	   90° for 6 m
	   180° for 14 m
		3 Starting point 3
		   45° for 21 m
		   90° for 5 m
		   180° for 15 m

Game 2A Card 4	Game 2A Card 5	Game 2A Card 6

1 Starting point 4
   0° for 15 m
   45° for 6 m
   225° for 21 m
	1 Starting point 5
	   0° for 10 m
	   270° for 10 m
	   225° for 14 m
		1 Starting point 6
		   0° for 18 m
		   270° for 7 m
		   225° for 25.5 m

2 Starting point 4
   0° for 5 m
   45° for 14 m
   180° for 15 m
	2 Starting point 5
	   0° for 18 m
	   270° for 2 m
	   225° for 25.5 m
		2 Starting point 6
		   45° for 7 m
		   270° for 25 m
		   225° for 7 m

3 Starting point 4
   315° for 10.5 m
   45° for 10.5 m
   135° for 21 m
	3 Starting point 5
	   45° for 14 m
	   315° for 7 m
	   225° for 21 m
		3 Starting point 6
		   315° for 14 m
		   90° for 15 m
		   180° for 10 m

Answers – Card 2A

Card 1		Card 2		Card 3		Card 4		Card 5		Card 6	
1	1–5	1	2–5	1	3–7	1	4–1	1	5–1	1	6–1
2	1–3	2	2–6	2	3–4	2	4–6	2	5–1	2	6–1
3	1–7	3	2–6	3	3–7	3	4–7	3	5–3	3	6–7

Game 2B Card 1	Game 2B Card 2	Game 2B Card 3

1 Starting point 1
   360° for 10 m
   East for 10 m
   135° for 14 m
	1 Starting point 2
	   360° for 2 m
	   North-East for 21 m
	   180° for 17 m
		1 Starting point 3
		   360° for 6 m
		   90° for 14 m
		   South-East for 8.5 m

2 Starting point 1
   360° for 4 m
   North-East for 14 m
   180° for 14 m
	2 Starting point 2
	   360° for 15 m
	   90° for 5 m
	   South-East for 21 m
		2 Starting point 3
		   360° for 10 m
		   North-East for 7 m
		   180° for 15 m

3 Starting point 1
   45° for 21 m
   East for 14 m
   180° for 16 m
	3 Starting point 2
	   45° for 20 m
	   90° for 6 m
	   180° for 14 m
		3 Starting point 3
		   45° for 21 m
		   90° for 5 m
		   180° for 15 m

Game 2B Card 4	Game 2B Card 5	Game 2B Card 6

1 Starting point 4
   360° for 10 m
   South-West for 21 m
   South-West for 21 m
	1 Starting point 5
	   360° for 18 m
	   270° for 10 m
	   South-West for 14 m
		1 Starting point 6
		   360° for 15 m
		   270° for 7 m
		   South-West for 25.5 m

2 Starting point 4
   360° for 5 m
   North-East for 14 m
   180° for 15 m
	2 Starting point 5
	   360° for 10 m
	   270° for 2 m
	   South-West for 25.5 m
		2 Starting point 6
		   45° for 7 m
		   270° for 25 m
		   South-West for 7 m

3 Starting point 4
   315° for 10.5 m
   North-East for 10.5 m
   135° for 21 m
	3 Starting point 5
	   45° for 14 m
	   North-West for 7 m
	   225° for 21 m
		3 Starting point 6
		   North-West for 14 m
		   90° for 15 m
		   180° for 10 m

Answers – Card 2B

Card 1	Card 2	Card 3	Card 4	Card 5	Card 6
1 1–5	1 2–5	1 3–7	1 4–1	1 5–1	1 6–1
2 1–3	2 2–6	2 3–4	2 4–6	2 5–1	2 6–1
3 1–7	3 2–6	3 3–7	3 4–7	3 5–3	3 6–7

SUBJECT INDEX

All Aboard	15
Auditory Direction	17
Basic Knots	39, 124, 125
Basic Lashings	130
Bearing and Clue Course	102, 103
Bearing and Distance Course	104, 105
Bearing from a Map	92, 101
Birds	23
Blindfold Order	111
Bushcraft	70, 71, 72, 120, 121, 122, 123
Bush Telephone	122
Campfire	71
Classification	50, 51
Colour in Maps	58
Compass Games	96, 100, 101, 141–148
Compass Use	62, 63, 64, 88
Compass Walk	66, 86
Develop Thinking	14
Develop Courses	35
Direction	56
Distance Ready Reckoner	95, 142–143
Electric Fence	112
Environmental Awareness	4, 5, 6, 7
Environmental Search	48, 49
Environmental Studies	20, 21, 22, 23, 48, 49, 50, 51, 52, 53, 74, 75, 76 77, 78
Fire Lighting	70, 72
Gardens	77
Grasses	21
Grid Reference	108, 109

Group Trail	28
Home	10
Hook Up	44
Initiative Activities	111, 112, 113
Insects	22
Knots	39, 68, 124, 125, 137–140
Knots and Bridges	126
Lashing Constructions	132, 133, 134, 135
Legend	61
Limited Legs	113
Local Environment	36
Man-made Signs	78
Mapping	10, 11, 12, 30, 32, 33, 34, 35, 36, 37, 38, 54, 55, 56, 57, 58, 59, 60, 61, 79, 80, 81, 82, 83, 84, 85, 86, 87
Map from Dictation	87
Map of Locality	81
Map Grid Course	109, 110
Mapping Representations	57
Morse Code	118, 119
Navigation	62, 63, 64, 65, 66, 67, 88, 89, 90, 91, 92, 93, 94, 95, 96, 99, 100, 101, 102, 103, 104, 105, 106, 107, 108, 109, 110
Nature Trail	52, 53
Observation	7
Observation Trail	37, 59
Observation Walk	12, 32
Photo Trail	27
Planning Mapping	54
Point-to-point Bearings	93
Poisonous Jelly	16
Position Change	43
Problem-solving	14, 15, 16, 17, 18, 43, 44, 45
Rocks	75
Ropes	39, 41, 68, 69, 124, 125, 126, 127, 128, 129, 130, 132, 133, 134, 135
Rope Bridges	41, 69, 127, 128, 129
Route Choice in Travel	94
Route to School	38
Rules in the Bush	13
Rules when Walking	6
Safety	13, 29

Scale	82, 83
Scale Map of Local Features	85
Scale Map of the School	84
School	38
School Map	55, 84
Schoolground	30
Search Patterns	29
Semaphore Code	114– 115, 116
Sensory	4, 5
Sensory Trail	76
Signalling	114, 116, 117, 118, 119
Sketch Map Course	33, 34 , 106, 107
Soil	74
String Trail	25
Symbols	79, 80
Tent Pitching	120, 121
The Four Pointer	45
Trailing	8, 9, 24, 25, 26, 27, 28, 37, 52, 53, 59, 60, 76
Treasure Hunt	26
Trees	20
Trolley	42
Unnatural	18
Walk a Bearing	89, 90, 91
Water Collection	123

www.ingramcontent.com/pod-product-compliance
Lightning Source LLC
Chambersburg PA
CBHW050240120526
44590CB00016B/2166